Lyman Abbott, und Andere

The Prophets of the Christian Faith

Lyman Abbott, und Andere

The Prophets of the Christian Faith

ISBN/EAN: 9783337126957

Printed in Europe, USA, Canada, Australia, Japan

Cover: Foto ©Lupo / pixelio.de

More available books at **www.hansebooks.com**

THE PROPHETS OF THE
CHRISTIAN FAITH

THE PROPHETS

OF

THE CHRISTIAN FAITH

BY THE

REV. LYMAN ABBOTT, REV. FRANCIS BROWN, REV. GEORGE MATHESON, REV. MARCUS DODS, REV. A. C. McGIFFERT, VERY REV. W. H. FREMANTLE, PROFESSOR ADOLF HARNACK, REV. A. M. FAIRBAIRN, REV. T. T. MUNGER, REV. A. V. G. ALLEN, AND VERY REV. F. W. FARRAR

New York
THE MACMILLAN COMPANY
LONDON: MACMILLAN & CO., Ltd.
1896

All rights reserved

COPYRIGHT, 1896,
BY THE MACMILLAN COMPANY.

Norwood Press
J. S. Cushing & Co. — Berwick & Smith
Norwood Mass. U.S.A.

CONTENTS

		PAGE
I.	WHAT IS A PROPHET?	1

By the Rev. LYMAN ABBOTT, D.D., Pastor of Plymouth Church, Brooklyn.

| II. | ISAIAH AS A PREACHER | 17 |

By the Rev. FRANCIS BROWN, D.D., Professor in Union Theological Seminary, New York.

| III. | THE APOSTLE PAUL | 33 |

By the Rev. GEORGE MATHESON, D.D., Pastor of St. Bernard's Church, Edinburgh, Scotland.

| IV. | CLEMENT OF ALEXANDRIA | 49 |

By the Rev. MARCUS DODS, D.D., Professor of New Testament Exegesis in New College, Edinburgh, Scotland.

| V. | ST. AUGUSTINE AS A PROPHET | 65 |

By the Rev. ARTHUR C. McGIFFERT, D.D., Professor of Church History in Union Theological Seminary, New York.

| VI. | JOHN WYCLIFFE | 81 |

By the Very Rev. W. H. FREMANTLE, D.D., Dean of Ripon.

| VII. | MARTIN LUTHER, THE PROPHET OF THE REFORMATION | 107 |

By Professor ADOLF HARNACK.

Contents

		PAGE
VIII.	JOHN WESLEY	123
	By the Very Rev. F. W. FARRAR, D.D., Dean of Canterbury.	
IX.	JONATHAN EDWARDS	145
	By the Rev. A. M. FAIRBAIRN, D.D., Principal of Mansfield College, Oxford, England.	
X.	HORACE BUSHNELL	167
	By the Rev. T. T. MUNGER, D.D.	
XI.	FREDERICK DENISON MAURICE . .	193
	By the Rev. A. V. G. ALLEN, D.D.	
XII.	CAN WE BE PROPHETS? . . .	215
	By the Very Rev. F. W. FARRAR, D.D., Dean of Canterbury.	

I
WHAT IS A PROPHET?

PROPHETS OF THE CHRISTIAN FAITH

I

WHAT IS A PROPHET?

BY THE REV. LYMAN ABBOTT, D.D.

"Just as a dumb or retired person," says Ewald, "must have a speaker to speak for him and declare his thoughts, so must God, who is dumb with respect to the mass of men, have his messenger or speaker; and hence the word [prophet], in its sacred sense, denotes him who speaks not of himself, but as commissioned by his God." Accepting this general definition, the prophet is an interpreter of God to men; he is not so much a foreteller as a forthteller. He receives his message from the Eternal and gives it as the messenger of the Eternal. The difference between the prophet and the priest is far more radical than Carlyle has represented it to be in his "Heroes and Hero-Worship." The priest interprets man to God. The office of priesthood assumes that God is too holy for ordinary mortals to approach; that some special persons must be appointed to mediate between man and God and approach God in lieu of, or in behalf of, man. He who believes that God is the All-Father, and that his ear is open to the faintest cry of his feeblest child, will have no place in his thoughts for any such mediator between man and his God. The office of the prophet is quite different. The need of a prophet grows, not out of the inaccessibility of God, but out of the imperfection of men. It is not — in this I venture to differ with Ewald, at least in phraseology — because God is dumb, but because man is deaf. Man lives so in the sphere of the material, he is so dependent upon the senses as a medium of communication, that he cannot appreciate, cannot understand, can hardly even receive, a message which is not translated into words. He is, indeed, the recipient of certain vague impressions, but he cannot interpret their meaning. He requires some one to interpret them to him, to embody them in language, to explain himself to himself, and so to make God and God's message clear to him. There is something like this in literature, art, and music. The poet, the artist, the musician, are each a kind of prophet. In all men there is some poetic nature, some dim perception of truth and beauty felt rather than perceived; sometimes it is not even felt, there is only a potentiality of feeling. The poet, by his expression, develops this potentiality, brings forth this hidden and sub-conscious life into consciousness, enables the soul to perceive what it could not perceive without this poetic interpreter. So the artist awakens the dormant sense of beauty, by presenting beauty to the sense-perception of men who were incapable of perceiving it by pure imagination; and the musician evokes musical life in souls incapable of responding to unheard music. Similarly, in every soul there is a possibility of divine life, a half-conscious recognition of truth and duty, of purity and love, of goodness and God. The prophet utters what unprophetic souls only vaguely feel, and thus vitalizes their feeling and converts it into will, purpose, action.

Prophecy, then, assumes that God is ever

brooding his children, awakening in them a life higher than their own, leading them up into life and light, as the sun leads up the plant from the darkness of the soil into the light of day. Some men are hardly conscious of this divine life; others are conscious of it only on rare occasions; some possess it as a vague, uninterpreted feeling, an enigmatical, restless desire for they know not what, a dream from which they seem to themselves to be continually awakening to the stern realities of life, a half-seen vision which disappears before it is really discerned; while to some it is the dominant force of their lives, the directing purpose, the rudder-holding hand, the great reality. Among these last, those who have the power to phrase this divine life in words, to interpret it so as to make its meaning clear to their fellows, are the world's prophets. They receive their message from God, and give it to their fellow-men.

Thus the prophets interpret God to man. But they also interpret man to himself. They explain to him what was before enigmatical in his own aspirations. They make legible the before invisible writing in his own experience. Every man is at times vaguely conscious of an unknown tongue speaking within himself. The prophets translate this unknown tongue. And no less do they interpret the age to itself. They see, not always, not generally, with infallible accuracy, but more clearly than their less spiritually-minded fellows, what is the meaning of the age, what the providential purpose which is in process of fulfilment, what its divine trend, what its great issues are sure to be. And because the object of their speech is to prepare men for these issues by interpreting to them this providential purpose, their forthtelling is also a foretelling. The prophet is not a mere historian; he is a historian only for the purpose of interpretation, and an interpreter only for the purpose of leadership. For his purpose is always to lead the people forth, to enable them to understand God's will in order that they may do God's work.

The prophet, therefore, is always a combination of piety and sympathy. A recluse is never truly a prophet. The mere man of action is never truly a prophet. He must be both a man of his time and a man of eternity. He is to interpret God to the men of his age; he must, therefore, understand both God and the men of his age. He is to translate the language of heaven into the language of earth; he must, therefore, understand both languages. He must, accordingly, first of all be what the Bible calls him, a "man of God," that is, a man whose life is born of God and comes forth from God. He must walk with God, live with God, commune with God, or he cannot understand God's message. He must go up into Mount Sinai with Moses, up into the Mount of Transfiguration with Christ. He must be at times absolutely alone with his God to receive God's message. But it is not enough that he receive the message; he must also be able to impart it. Not every spiritually-minded man is a prophet. He must also understand men — the men of his own age, their lives, their experiences, their needs. The prophets, therefore, belong to no class or order. Rarely has one been taken from any select circle, whether ecclesiastical or social. Moses was a herdsman, David a shepherd, Isaiah a peasant's son. When one is found in the hierarchy, this very fact limits his usefulness; Ezekiel is not so widely read nor so widely useful as the Great Unknown. The school of the prophets produces no prophets. They cannot be created by educational processes. Education may add to their equipment, but it is not and cannot be the secret of their power. That lies in the possession of this twofold faculty — the hearing ear and the speaking mouth; the ear to hear God, the mouth to speak to man; the understanding of God's message, and the capacity to impart it to men who have not understood it.

It is a mistake to suppose that the prophet is always, or even generally, the bearer of a new message to the world. This he may sometimes be, but more generally he interprets to a wider circle a truth before known only to a few; or makes vital in life a truth which before was only a philosophical opinion; or restores to human consciousness a truth it had lost; or puts into new and better perspective a truth which had been suffered to lie forgotten in the background; or carries on to its legitimate and necessary conclusions truths whose issue and meaning the world had not seen; or makes new applications of familiar truths. The few philosophers of Egypt believed that there was one God above all gods; Moses brought this truth out of its hiding-place in the schools and made it the foundation of a new State and the inspiration of a new worship. This prophet of the Law taught that God is one, that he is a righteous God, and that he requires righteousness of his children. This is the burden of the Book of the Covenant, which is probably the oldest writing in the Bible, and of Deuteronomy, which, whatever its date as a manuscript, embodies the prophetic message of Moses, the great Lawgiver. David brought into the foreground the truth that God is merciful, sang of a Father who pities his children, and handed down to future generations, as his bequest to them, the revelation embodied in the phrase " The sure mercies of David." Elijah proclaimed nothing new; he simply retold the story of the past — one God, just and merciful; he was the prophet of a restoration. The Great Unknown — the second Isaiah — himself taught by the years of captivity in Babylon that the spirit of righteousness and reverence is not confined within any geographical boundaries, saw clearly that if there is but one God, ever righteous and merciful, then his law extends over all nations and his mercy is provided for all; he was the prophet of a catholic religion.

It is equally a mistake to suppose that prophecy ceased and prophets were no more after the coming of Christ. It is true that a chief message of the Old Testament prophets, from Moses to Malachi, is that a Messiah is yet to come; and, of course, after he had come, this theme, as one of foretelling, ceased forever. What had been prophecy became history. The Incarnation, which had been a vision and a hope, became a fact witnessed to by the senses: a somewhat concerning which the Apostle could write, "which we have seen with our eyes, which we have looked upon, and our hands have handled of the Word of life." But in the larger sense of a forthtelling — a spiritual perception, and an effective interpretation — prophecy has not ceased, and will not, until every eye shall see Him face to face. A wider range of prophecy, not its cessation, is anticipated by Joel as the result of the Incarnation. The secret of prophecy is imparted by Christ to the Apostles when he breathes upon them; the promise of prophecy, when he promises the Holy Spirit to guide them into all truth; the commission to prophesy, in the command, "What ye hear in the ear, that proclaim ye upon the housetops." Prophets are mentioned in the Book of Acts as recognized teachers in the Apostolic Church, and are included by Paul in his list of its ministers; and the preacher's recipient faith is accounted by him as at once the measure and the secret of the prophet's forthtelling. To deny to the Christian Church prophets, to assume that prophecy ceased with the close of the New Testament canon, to draw a sharp line between the prophets before and the prophets subsequent to the first century, appears to me to foster two errors: one, that which imputes to the Hebrew prophets an infallibility which they never claimed for themselves; the other, to deny to the Church since Christ that presence of a living, speaking, interpreted God, which was characteristic of the Hebrew Church, and which Christ distinctly and emphatically declared should continue to be characteristic of the Christian Church.

In a true sense, every real preacher is a prophet. If he is not a prophet, if he does not receive a message direct from God which he can communicate to man, if he is not a forthteller, an interpreter, a divine messenger, he is no true preacher. In one respect he has an immeasurable advantage which the earlier prophets did not possess. His message he can always compare with the life and teachings of his Master, and thus determine whether it is in very truth a divine message or only a human phantasy. His message will sometimes, perhaps generally, be a simple re-enunciation of that which other Christian prophets have given or are giving; but it will have no real prophetic power unless it has come to him from his Father, for he can prophesy only according to the proportion of his faith, only as what he has heard in the ear he is proclaiming from the pulpit. But while thus every Christian preacher may be and should be a prophet, an interpreter of the mystic voice of God to the men of his generation, there have been pre-eminent prophets in the Christian Church as there were in the Hebrew Church, men whose message has had all the force of a new revelation, men whose faith vitalized truths that were before held as mere inert opinions, or revived truths that had been forgotten, or revealed — that is, unveiled — truths to the common people which had been concealed in the closets of the few, or made new applications of familiar truths to new and unfamiliar conditions of life. These men are as truly prophets, interpreters, forthtellers, as Isaiah, Jeremiah, or Ezekiel. Such was Clement of Alexandria, with his message of the divine immanence; Augustine, with his message of divine sovereignty from the authority of which no man can escape; Luther, with his message of personal responsibility to God and therefore personal freedom from all who interpose themselves between the soul and God; John Wesley, with his message that the Christian religion is the universal religion, adapted to all sorts and conditions of men; Jonathan Edwards, with his revived statement of the combined messages of Clement and Augustine, divine sovereignty and divine indwelling; Swedenborg, with his message that religion is life, not ritual or dogma; Maurice, with his message of a living God as the Father of whom the whole family in heaven and on earth is named; Bushnell, with his message of the transcendent character of spiritual experience and the inadequacy of all creeds, traditions, and theologies to give expression to it; Channing, with his message that man is God's son, however far he may have wandered from his Father's house; Finney, with his message to a paralyzed Church bound in the chains of a fatalistic philosophy, "All things are possible to him that believeth"; Henry Ward Beecher, with his message summoning the Puritan Church from bowing awe-stricken at the foot of Mount Sinai to clasp love-stricken the cross on Calvary; Phillips Brooks, with his message of the universal presence and grace of God and the abundance of life in and through his indwelling — these and many others have been true prophets of the Christian Church. Every such man seeing the need of humanity, receiving his message from God and giving it as God's interpreter to God's children — a son of man, but no less a son of God, sent by God to be a forthteller of God's word, in whatever age or community he may live, however large or small his audience, however fresh or familiar his message, is a prophet of the living God.

II

ISAIAH AS A PREACHER

II

ISAIAH AS A PREACHER

BY THE REV. FRANCIS BROWN, D.D.

MUCH depends on our understanding the relation of the prophets to their own times. It is difficult for some good people to learn that this is of primary consequence — only less fundamental than their close relation to God. The importance they have for us rests very largely on the more direct importance they had for their own contemporaries. No intelligent person now supposes that prediction is all of prophecy, but many intelligent persons fail to perceive or to appreciate the fact that, in God's ordering, predictive prophecy is conditioned by the circumstances that attended its birth, and is designed to affect contemporary belief and life. The same thing is true of the moral and religious teachings of the prophets. The prophets were not moral philosophers nor systematic theologians. Neither the speculative nor the scientific spirit controlled them. They had visions, but they were not visionaries; they taught great truths, but they were not professors of dogmatics. They were men of intense spiritual life, eager to influence the national organism of which they themselves formed a part — the men and women among whom they moved, whose wants and sins they clearly saw. They were not essayists nor theorizers. They were preachers and interpreters. From the stern announcements of Amos and the passionate pleadings of Hosea, down to the fierce joy of Nahum over Nineveh's fall, the melancholy of Jeremiah at his people's calamity, and the encouragements and spiritual exhortations of Haggai, Zechariah, and Malachi, they are all men of their own people, with throbbing, longing hearts. Even the apocalyptic prophets, such as Ezekiel, Joel, and Daniel, make present conditions their starting-point. It is this which, humanly speaking, gives to their messages their permanent vitality. Conditions and circumstances change, but the living God and the heart of man abide, and those who have ever really interpreted the one to the other are the preachers of all time.

As soon as we recognize the prophets as children and servants of their own age, the study of that age and its various periods and experiences becomes imperative. We cannot understand them without knowing the character and needs of their people at the time when they spoke. The better we know these — the more minutely we learn the fitness of prophetic utterances to the exact situations that called them forth — the richer will these utterances become for us, not only as memorials of a past age, but also, and especially, as messages to ourselves.

No prophet illustrates all this better than that most gifted of the prophets, Isaiah. Isaiah was a man of great natural endowments, intensified and consecrated to the loftiest ends by his self-surrender to God. He had the intellectual grasp of a great statesman, and the fervid imagination of a great poet. He could make combinations and foresee consequences, and warn him who ventured upon devious ways; he could portray with sustained power, he could overwhelm with the outpourings of righteous indignation, he could pierce with irony, he could cheapen with ridicule, he could mourn over his self-destroying people, he could sympathize with the downcast, he could rise to heights of spiritual experience and anticipation. All his gifts were in the service of his generation. He was absorbed in them, and in God's dealings with them. The present was awful to him because of its issues for them; the future was gloomy because it held punishment for their obstinacy, or bright because after the purification was to come their glory and their peace.

Fortunately for us, in the case of no other prophet have we a better opportunity to learn the concrete character of his thought, or study the influences which shaped its expression.[1] While our information is only to a slight degree of a personal character, and while our knowledge of the contemporary history is not equally full at all points, we find that there were two crises in the national life around which many of Isaiah's most telling sermons group themselves — the Syro-Ephraimistic war (B.C. 734 ff.), with the Assyrian campaign under Tiglathpileser III., by which that war

---

[1] Among recent writers in English on this subject may be named Canon S. R. Driver, D.D., "Isaiah, His Life and Times," 2d Ed., 1893; Professor George Adam Smith, D.D., "The Book of Isaiah," Vol. I., 1889; Canon T. K. Cheyne, D.D., "Introduction to the Book of Isaiah," 1895; Professor Maximilian Lindsay Kellner, "The Prophecies of Isaiah: An Outline Study," 1895.

was terminated, and the invasion of Sennacherib, B.C. 701. Lack of exact chronological arrangement in our present Isaian collection makes the assignment of the various addresses and sermons more difficult than it otherwise would be, but scholars are fairly well agreed as to the illustrations here given.

As so frequently happens under autocratic rule, the humiliation of Judah under Ahaz followed speedily upon the military successes of Uzziah and Jotham — Ahaz's grandfather and father. The bold leader and strong ruler passes away, a weakling succeeds him, and there is no habit of self-control, self-reliance, and responsible patriotism in the many, to take the place of the one vigorous hand. Probably the earliest words of Isaiah preserved to us are those in which he characterized the moral condition of Judah at the close of Jotham's reign and the beginning of that of Ahaz, about the year 735. Conquest had brought increase of wealth, luxury, pride, idolatry, looseness of life, weakening of moral fibre. The inevitable consequences of this emasculation could not be hidden from the keen eye of Isaiah, divinely clarified, and sweeping the horizon, upon which the might of Assyria was distinctly looming up.

Accusation and warning have seldom been addressed to a nation in nobler and more searching language than that preserved to us — in a somewhat fragmentary form, it is true — in Isa. ii. 6–21. After the arraignment, vv. 6 ff., comes the announcement of the judgment day of Yahweh, vv. 12 ff.:

> For a day hath Yahweh Sebaoth
> Upon all that is exalted and high,
> And upon all that is uplifted, — yea it shall be laid low, —
> And upon all the cedars of Lebanon,
> And upon all the oaks of Bashan.
> And upon all the high mountains,
> And upon all the uplifted hills,
> And upon every tower that is lofty,
> And upon every fortified wall,
> And upon all Tarshish ships,
> And upon all the objects of delight,
> And the haughtiness of man shall be abased,
> And brought low the loftiness of men,
> And Yahweh alone shall be exalted
> In that day!

The early part of the third chapter contains the prophet's scourging attack on the political condition of the people under the weak and effeminate rule of Ahaz.

For behold! the Lord, Yahweh Sebaoth,
Removeth from Jerusalem and from Judah support and stay,
Hero and man of war, judge and prophet,
And diviner and elder, captain of fifty and exalted one,
And counsellor and skilful magician and shrewd enchanter,
And I will set boys as their princes, and children shall rule over them (vv. 1-4).
My people, its overseer is a wilful child,
And women, they have ruled over it;
My people, those guiding thee are misleading,
And the way of thy paths they have swallowed up (v. 12).

In the latter part of the same chapter comes the intense and contemptuous ridicule of the luxurious and worthless women of the court. In chapter v. 8 ff., we find a group of "Woes" pronounced upon oppression, intemperance, and reckless presumption, and at the beginning of the same chapter a statement of the whole case of Yahweh against Israel, in which sternness is joined with profound and tender sadness:

What was there more to do for my vineyárd that I did not in it?

Why did I expect it to bear grape-clusters, and it bore worthless things?

Chapter vii., which begins in narrative form, shows us the invasion of Pekah and Rezin already in progress, and the prophet vainly endeavouring to awaken faith in God in the heart of the superficial and faint-hearted Ahaz, who appears already to have formed the plan of saving himself from the allied enemies, Aram and northern Israel, by throwing himself into the arms of Assyria, as related in 2 Kings xvi. All Isaiah's assurances are of no avail, not even his declaration that deliverance is so certain and will be so speedy that a child soon to be born shall by right receive the name "God-with-us," because the hand of God shall by that time already be manifest in the defeat of the foe. Ahaz is too timid and too far involved with Tiglathpileser to respond, and the prophet is compelled to pass in vv. 17 ff. to an announcement of the disaster that will follow upon the Assyrian alliance.

To a time a little later, when Assyria was already on the move, belongs the declaration of judgment upon the Northern Kingdom, ix. 8–21, winding up with the magnificent description of the oncoming Assyrian host, v. 26–30, which has become displaced:

And he hath lifted up a signal to the nations afar, and hath hissed to him at the end of the earth,
And behold, hastily, swiftly, he cometh!
None weary, and none stumbling among them,— he slumbereth not and he sleepeth not.
And the girdle of his loins hath not been loosed, and the thong of his sandals not broken!
Whose arrows are sharpened, and all his bows bent;
The hoofs of his horses, like flint are they reckoned, and his wheels like the whirlwind!
A roar he hath like the lion, he roareth like the young lions,
And he growleth, and he seizeth prey, and he carrieth it safe away, and there is none that delivereth,
And he growleth over them in that day, like the growling of the sea,
And they look to earth, and lo, thick darkness, and the light hath grown dark in its clouds!
[For all this his wrath has not turned back, and still is his hand stretched forth!]

About the second great crisis of Jerusalem during Isaiah's ministry, that caused by the invasion of Sennacherib in 701, another set of prophecies group themselves. In these, although the people is not freed from blame for the perils of the situation, especially in respect to the false move of intrigue with Egypt, the general tone is more cheerful, and the expectancy of deliverance more absolute. This time the King (Hezekiah) and the prophet were in more substantial accord. The words of Isaiah contained in 2 Kings xix. 6, 7, 20 ff. (= Isa. xxxvii. 6, 7, 21 ff.), indicate the hopeful tenor of what he then felt moved to say. From a somewhat earlier year are chapters xxix., xxx., xxxi., xxxii.; more nearly coincident in time are the verses xiv. 1-14. For our purposes the prophecy concerning Assyria, x. 5 ff., may be cited. The point of view is different from that of ix. 7 ff., v. 26 ff. Here the presumption and the punishment of Assyria is set in the foreground, and assurance is given to Jerusalem of rescue from this seemingly invincible foe.

Ho, Asshur! rod of mine anger! yea, a staff in their hand is my wrath!
Against a profane nation do I send him, and over the people of my rage do I command him!

To take spoil and seize booty, and to make them a trampling, like mire in the streets.
But he, not so doth he devise, and his heart, not so doth it reckon.
For to destroy (is) in his heart, and to cut off nations, not a few.
For he saith, Are not my princes altogether kings? Is not Calno as Carchemish?
Or is not Hamath as Arpad, or is not Samaria as Damascus?
As my hand hath lighted upon the kingdoms of the no-gods,—and their images are more than in Jerusalem,—
Shall I not, as I have done to Samaria and her no-gods, so do to Jerusalem and her idols?

But Yahweh shall punish him for his presumption. The passage ends with the imaginative picture of the approach of the Assyrian army to Jerusalem from the north, and its sudden overthrow (vv. 28–34):

He hath come upon Ayyath, hath passed by Migron, at Michmash he storeth his baggage;
They have crossed the pass, at Geba they have taken night-quarters.
Ramah trembleth, Gibeah of Saul hath fled.
Cry aloud, daughter of Gallim, give ear, Layisha, answer her, Anathoth!

Madmenah hath become a wanderer, the dwellers in Gebim have hurried off (their treasures).
This very day he is to halt in Nob, brandishing his hand against the mountain of the daughter of Zion;
Behold, the Lord, Yahweh Sebaoth, loppeth off the boughs with frightful crash,
And the high in stature are hewn down, and the lofty, they shall be laid low;
And he shall cut down the thickets of the forest with iron, and Lebanon by a mighty one shall fall!

There is space now for only a word about the specific Messianic predictions ascribed to Isaiah — those in which the expectation of a great deliverance involves a future king to be the great deliverer. These, too, are rooted, more or less distinctly, in the present, and their expression is framed for effect upon the prophet's own contemporaries. Scholars generally hold that the most definite and stirring of them all found its point of contact with the national life in the devastation of northeast Israel by Tiglathpileser III., in the invasion of 734, which cost Pekah his throne and his life. It was then that Isaiah, keenly feeling the blow which had fallen upon the sister kingdom, recognizing, indeed, the divine mission of Assyria, but believing this to be only temporary, and confident that the haughty invader must be overthrown, despairing of any leadership in that overthrow on the part of the weak, timorous, and self-willed Ahaz, received power to announce the birth of the child who was to conquer all enemies, set his people free, and secure them peace. All the world knows the verses now, and gives them a comprehensive and spiritual interpretation, but the political conditions of Isaiah's time have left an indelible mark upon them, and we can interpret them largely because he compressed into them so much intensity of patriotic feeling and so much confidence of faith. I am speaking of the great prediction of ix. 1–6, ending with the stanza (vv. 4–6):

Yea, every boot of the man that stampeth with noise, and garment rolled in blood —
It shall be for burning, — fuel for fire.
For a child is born to us, a son is given to us, and the dominion shall come upon his shoulder,
And his name shall be called Wonder of a Counsellor, God-hero, Possessor of Spoil, Prince of Peace!
For the increase of the dominion and for peace without end, upon the throne of David and over his kingdom,

Establishing it and sustaining it, by justice and by righteousness, from now, even forever!
The zeal of Yahweh Sebaoth will perform this.

This portrayal of Isaiah's prophetic work has been meagre enough. Into some regions of his thought it has not been possible even to enter. But the illustrations given are sufficient to establish his greatness—greatness as an artist and greatness as a preacher. His sermons are poems, in which poetic fire and skill are wholly genuine and wholly at the service of his moral integrity and his spiritual insight, so that through them God revealed his will to the men of Isaiah's time, and has revealed his will afresh to the successive generations since Isaiah died.

III

THE APOSTLE PAUL

III

THE APOSTLE PAUL

BY THE REV. GEORGE MATHESON, D.D.

THE figures of the New Testament are representative men; each stands for some phase of the soul. Matthew is the type of conservatism, "that it might be fulfilled." Mark is the symbol of present action, "straightway he commanded." Luke is the embodiment of human sympathy. John is the love of the ideal. Nathaniel is the child; Nicodemus is the student; Peter is the youth; Thomas is the reflective and somewhat careworn man. No portrait in this gallery is without its special significance.

What is Paul? It seems at first sight equivalent to asking "What is Shakespeare?" It appears as if the only word which would describe him is myriad-mindedness. And yet, to my mind, the remarkable feature about Paul is not variety but unity — not the diversity of his experiences, but the one thread which connects them. If I were asked to state in a single phrase what Paul represents, I would say, "The pilgrim's progress." I would say that his life, as indicated in the historical order of his epistles, describes the normal course through which each Christian is to journey in his passage from the scene of shadows into the happy land of Beulah.

I say, "the *normal* course." But the point I wish to emphasize is that to Paul himself it was very abnormal. He was the initiator of that which has since become chronic and habitual. The course proposed for the Old Testament pilgrims was the very opposite of that prescribed for Paul. Theirs was a march from the desert into the promised land; Paul's was a progress from the promised land into the desert. They began with the valley, passed up to the plain, and ended on the height; he began with the height, passed down to the plain, and ended with the valley. They proceeded from law to love; he descended from love to law. They set up their ladder on the earth and tried to reach the heavens; he fixed his ladder in the heavens and tried to reach the earth.

It was not only from the men of the Old Testament that Paul was thus distinguished; his experience was equally marked out from the original Apostles — the men of transition between the old and the new. These proceeded from the human to the divine. They gazed first on the Christ of the flesh. They followed the steps of the Son of man from the cradle to the cross; when the crown came, their pilgrimage was over. But Paul began with the crown. His first sight of the Christ was the Christ glorified. He knew the power of His resurrection before he felt the fellowship of His sufferings. His progress was a progress backward. He had begun with the light of immortality; he had to retrace his steps to take up the life of time. It was an abnormal experience, though it was to become universal. He was the first of the new régime, and for a while the only one. He says he was "born out of due time." I understand him to mean, not that he was born too late, but that he was born too soon. He claimed to have a vision of the Christian life which was above his age, before his day, in advance of his contemporaries. He claimed to be the follower of One whose progress had been from heaven to earth, who had begun with the form of God and ended with the form of a servant, who had emptied himself step by step into sympathy with things beneath him, and paused not, rested not, until he had made the human divine. The progress of St. Paul was like that of his Master — a progress downward.

He begins in the air — in the other world. He has been caught up to meet his Lord, and the earth disappears from his view. He sees nothing but the second advent; he hears nothing but the last trump. All perspective has vanished; the end is at the door. Christ is coming; in a little while he will be here. What is this world to any man? Before his descending shout of triumph its proudest pomps shall melt away. Before the first gaze of the man of Tarsus there floated the form of only one Christ — the Christ of resurrection. The light which smote him from heaven put out all the candles of earth. Everything below that sun became a thing of insignificance. The kingdoms of the world and the glory of them vanished like smoke. Their inhabitants became as grasshoppers, their events as waterdrops. The only bells heard were the bells of the New Jerusalem, and they summoned all men to a cathedral above.

Then there came a cloud; I know not when, I know not how. I only know it was somewhere between the Thessalonians and the Galatians. In his letter to Corinth he speaks of it as a thorn; in his letter to Rome he describes it as a warfare; both are introduced as retrospects of a dark, and to some extent a surmounted, past. The cause of the cloud I cannot tell; probably it was something external. But the main point is that it was something which made Paul feel himself less ready for his change. The second advent moves further off; the world looms nearer. He finds that the light which fell upon him at Damascus was like the deluge; it had only covered the old world — not annihilated it. There were two natures within him — Saul and Paul. For the first time in his life he felt thoroughly bad. What right had he to struggle? Had he not tasted of the heavenly gift; had he not seen the Lord? Where was the blessedness he had known in Arabia? Where was the joy with which he had written to Thessalonica? Where was the exultation with which he had been taken up to the third heaven? What was this that had come to him — this flesh lusting against the spirit, this law in his members warring against the law of his mind? Was not this spiritual death? The strong soul of yesterday beat upon his breast and cried, "O wretched man that I am!"

Then came a new gleam of glory, and it came, not from the third heaven, but from the very mist into which Paul had wandered. It brought a great message to his soul. It said: Your seeming fall is a rise. You are further removed from death now than you were in your hour of immediate vision. The true sign of spiritual life is spiritual dissatisfaction. There is nothing which justifies a man like his belief in the existence of a beauty which he himself cannot reach.

Paul has come a step down his ladder, which means a step up his pilgrimage. He has come nearer to the earth. He has passed from sight to faith — from an ideal of perfect satisfaction to an ideal which eludes him by its glory. But already another step was preparing. What was that glory in Christ which had hitherto eluded him? It was love. The moment Paul said, "I believe in love," he had put out his foot for a further step downward. Hitherto, however beautiful, his experience had been mainly personal. He had found rest to his own soul. But that is not the half of the Christian life. Paul's deepest Christianity was yet to come. He had begun with sight; his passage from the Thessalonians to the Galatians had been a passage from sight to faith; his passage from the Galatians to the Corinthians is a passage from faith to love. You say "it was a very short time in which to make such a transition." Yes; but the transitions of God's Spirit are, in their last result, almost momentary. I can well-nigh hear the very hour strike in which he passed over the line. The man who wrote the magnificent hymn of the thirteenth chapter of 1st Corinthians has made a leap; and when he touches the ground it is no longer the old ground, but a plane higher in God's sight, because lower in the sight of man.

Can you fail to observe that from this time onward the teaching of Paul takes another channel? It becomes less personal, more humanitarian. Even his view of predestination is to my mind the result of his new breadth, not of his old narrowness. He sees that a mother's love is always *predestinating* love. When a mother foreknows that her child is about to come into the world, even before its birth, she conforms it to an image; she figures to herself what she would like it to be. That is, in my opinion, the metaphor which glittered before the eyes of the great Apostle when he proclaimed that the All-Father had predestined his children "to be conformed to the image of his Son." Divine Love, foreknowing that its children were about to be born, ere ever they had a character, ere ever they had a being, planned for them a destiny of glory, figured them in the likeness of the most beautiful thing it knew, and said within itself, "I baptize them into the name of Jesus." Nay, was not baptism into Christ's name itself simply the predestination of love — the expression in the heart of the Divine Parent of a great, an unquenchable desire that the new convert should rise to heights altogether unearthly, and attain to nothing less than the image of the Son?

Paul has now reached what he himself calls the glory of the cross. He had begun with the crown — the sight of the Christ of resurrection. He had passed from sight to faith — the vision of an ideal which was beyond him, and after which he must strive. He has now come from faith to love — the perception that others have an ideal as well as he. Has Paul now arrived at the terminus? No. He has reached the knowledge that the cross is the glory of God; but there is a step beyond even that — he must "rejoice in *hope* of the glory of God." Faith in Christ was the parent of love, because it was the belief in love; but Paul makes the further discovery that love is the parent of hope. He says, in so many words, that the reason why he is not ashamed to hope is that the love of God is shed abroad in his heart (Romans v. 5). He was of a spirit not naturally sanguine; I have heard him called a pessimist. In his Epistle to the Thessalonians his main hope for the world seems to have been that a divine power is keeping things from being worse; and truly he was right. But when the enthusiasm of the cross burst upon him, hope had a deeper revelation to bring. We again hear the clock strike as he passes the line. He had spoken of justification by faith; he had called love "a more excellent way"; he was now to cry, "We are saved by *hope*." Love was the parent of hope. No doubt the parent was greater than the child; yet the child was indispensable to the support of the parent. And, with this latest birth in the soul of Paul, there comes a widening of his horizon. There is nothing which tells such tales as a letter, and often most in the things it does not say. Already in the Epistle to the Romans we begin to catch breezes — currents of air which apprise us that there is an opening somewhere not far away. As we advance beyond the boundaries of that Epistle, the current freshens. He tells the Philippians in express terms that the purpose of God's heart was that every man in every place should bend his knee in prayer. A few miles more and we are out in the open, with the gusts of the great sea around us. As we pass from the coasts of Philippi we are in a new element — an element of breadth, I had almost said of secularism, an element which increases in strength from the outpouring of the letter to Ephesus, until those notes of pastoral counsel which speak the last farewell.

What is this new element in Paul? I have called it secularism; it would be more correct to call it the extension of the sacred. Hitherto, Paul had seen in Christ merely the head of a body of members. But now he began to see more. Christ was the head of the Church, but was he not also head of the State — of all principalities and powers? Was not this magnificent Roman Empire, however unconsciously to itself, already the kingdom of God? Was not Cæsar as much the servant of Christ as *he* was, albeit he knew it not? Was this world a secular system at all? Was the distinction between Church and State a real one? would not the fulness of time show that all things had been " gathered together in Christ"? As he approached Rome, and as the spectacle of Roman unity swam before his eyes, he asked himself if Christ's kingdom would be less incorporative than this kingdom of man. He asked himself if this Roman unity was really the work of Cæsar, if it was not itself only a product of that divine order which had arranged thrones and principalities and powers. So asking, so thinking, Paul stepped into the world again. He came back to the haunts from which his conversion had lifted him; he claimed them for Christ. He found the land of Beulah on the earthly side. For the second time in his life he preached the things which once had been alien to him. Very beautiful to my mind is the passage, Ephesians iii. 14 and 15, in which he declares that the idea of family life is modelled after the relationship of the Father in heaven. Beautiful, because I think there was a time when Paul would not have said it — a time of storm and stress below, of dazzling light above, when the radiance of the heavenly vision had blinded him to earthly ties. Beautiful, too, because it is no accidental utterance. It is the keynote of his latest song. If his morning carol is to the Christ of the heavens, his evening lay is to the Christ of the home; if he begins with love on the wing, he ends with love in the nest. All his latest notes are of home.

I cannot better conclude than by placing side by side Paul's earliest and latest ideals of Christian joy — the one from his first letter, the other almost from his last. He says to the Thessalonians, "We shall be caught up together in the clouds to meet the Lord in the air"; he says to Titus, "The grace that bringeth salvation hath appeared unto all men, teaching to live soberly, righteously, and godly in this present world." Do I say that at the close of his pilgrimage he has found his first experience to be untrue? No; rather for the first time has he discovered its real value. He has found that the advantage of going up is the new strength we get for coming down. The bird that at dawn sings in the uplands may be heard in the afternoon on the ledge of an office wall; but the song on the office wall has been learned in the uplands. Moses had the vision of Nebo before coming down to the common lot of men ; but the vision of Nebo helped him to come down. Paul's first revelation was the sight of immortality, but the sight of immortality gave value to the earth ; and he who began with the vision of the ascending Christ was bound sooner or later to recognize the possibilities of "this present world."

IV

CLEMENT OF ALEXANDRIA

IV

CLEMENT OF ALEXANDRIA

BY THE REV. MARCUS DODS, D.D.

TITUS FLAVIUS CLEMENS, commonly known as Clement of Alexandria, may be accepted as the representative of Greek Theology. In some respects either Origen or Athanasius might more suitably stand as its exponent, but Clement has the advantage of being earlier than either of these great theologians, and of being Origen's teacher and predecessor as head of the catechetical school of Alexandria. "He stands in the same relation to those that came after him that Augustine sustained to the Latin theology of the Middle Ages, or Luther and Calvin to the later Protestantism."

Of his personal history little is known. He wrote in the reign of Severus (193-211 A.D.), and the probability is that he was born in Athens about the middle of the second century. In quest of truth he travelled in Italy,

Syria, and Asia Minor, until finally he "caught the true Sicilian bee," Pantænus in Alexandria. In a year or two afterwards he was ordained a presbyter of the Church, and succeeded Pantænus as Master of the Catechetical School. His residence in Alexandria undoubtedly had a great influence, not only on the form of his writings, but on his thought, and especially on his attitude towards philosophy. In this magnificent, busy, and dissipated city, every vice of heathenism and the most sumptuous and seductive idolatrous worship were daily obtruded on the notice of Clement. Everything that paganism had to attract, to delude, to bind, was matter of familiar observation to the man who was destined to become, not only the most voluminous, but in many respects the most sagacious and convincing, of Christian apologists.

In Alexandria Clement had also opportunity to acquire that learning which was essential to qualify him to meet the mental condition of religious inquirers in the second century. It was at least as important to gain to the new faith the philosophers and scholars of the museum as the mechanics of the docks and building-yards, or the warehouse porters. His office as teacher of the Christian school exposed him to the interrogation of all who had difficulties about the new religion. The cavils which were concocted by the wits of the museum, the theories which were broached in the dining-hall of the professors, would naturally find their way to the ears of Clement. And so he drew around the young plants which were under his charge the hedge, as he calls it, of a learning superior to that of the assailants. Excepting Athenæus, probably no ancient writer could be named who cites four hundred authors, but a larger number than this must measure the reading of Clement. This great learning he used, not for display, but as a missionary engine. His three great books, the "Protreptikos," the "Paidagogos," and the "Stromateis," written respectively for the heathen, the catechumen, and the Christian Gnostic, all bear witness to his zeal no less than to his knowledge.

In the apologetic of Clement we become aware that his conciliatory attitude is the result not merely of geniality of disposition, but of principle — the principle, to state it in his own words, that "there is one river of truth, but many streams fall into it on this side and on that." He believed that Philosophy had been in its measure a "schoolmaster" to the Greeks, as the Law had been to the Jews; and that even after the Advent it served as a preparatory training which might lead men to Christianity. By "philosophy," as he is careful to explain, he did not mean the teaching of any particular school, the Platonic, Aristotelian, or Epicurean, but whatever had been well said by any sect "which teaches righteousness along with science." As Justin had taught that the Logos had been the revealer of truth to the heathen philosophers, so Clement maintains that philosophy is God's gift to men "for the sake of those who not otherwise than by its means would abstain from what is evil."

This catholic tendency which is so marked a feature of the second century was no doubt stimulated, if not wholly caused, by the universalism of the Empire. As Professor Allen says, "The necessity of enforcing one common method of legal procedure upon a variety of peoples, each with its own conception of justice and of its practical administration, gave rise to the comprehensive spirit of Roman law and the endeavour to ground it in the nature of man. A similar necessity gave rise to similar efforts in the sphere of religious thought." The necessities of Clement's position also drove him to adopt his liberal views and methods. He expressly affirms that he felt himself impelled to become a Greek to the Greeks, and that in order to remove their difficulties he must first feel them, must recognize the truth they held before he could add to it, and must see their error from their own point of view. Never, on the other hand, does he allow it to be supposed that he considers philosophy to be a sufficient guide. Christ alone possesses the whole truth. There is only One who can perfectly satisfy, only One who can heal, purify, and restore to God.

In this teaching Clement is the type not only of one of the most remarkable phases of early Christianity, but he is the representative of a tendency or mental attitude which reappears in all ages of the history of Christendom. It would appear from unmistakable signs, in our own day, that the Church has not yet made up its mind to adopt Clement's theory of the relation of non-Christian religions and philosophies to Christianity. The Bampton Lecturer for 1894 (Mr. Illingworth), speaking of the non-Christian sacred books of the world, says: "With all their imperfection and manifest inferiority, there is that in them which we can well believe to have been a vehicle of divine teaching to the nations they addressed, and, if so, to have been inspired, as their possessors believed." And in confirmation of his statement he quotes Clement, who speaks to the same effect: "Perchance philosophy was given to the Greeks, directly and primarily, till the Lord should call the Greeks." And again, "The barbarian and Greek philosophy has torn off a fragment, not from the mythology of Dionysus, but from the theology of the Eternal Word." Yet the man who has done more for India and for Christianity in India than any other during this generation has been severely taken to task for pointing out that Hinduism has in it elements of good and a contribution to make to the Church and to the world.

St. Paul's method of dealing with the heathen, his addresses at Lystra and at Athens, should have made it impossible to deny that God has been training Gentile as well as Jew for Christ. And probably the idea that heathenism and all its works are wholly of the devil is pretty well obsolete. But there is still prevalent a lurking fear that in recognizing the good that is outside Christianity the supremacy and essential distinction of our religion may be lost. Instead of levelling up, a process of levelling down may be initiated. And even although this fear must not be allowed to blind us to the education of the world as a whole, and to the part played by the various races in that education, yet there are undoubtedly dangers to be avoided. For example, we see that in Clement this approximation of Christianity to philosophy caused him all but uniformly to present Christ as a teacher. With him redemption is little more than the reception of Christ's teaching, the soul being purified and, in the Platonic sense, redeemed by the truth. Fate comes to be nothing more than the mental acceptance of the revelation of Christ. The saving power of Christ consists in his manifestation of the Father's love. The idea of a redemption by expiation is quite in the background, and may easily be overlooked. Christ saves by the light he brings. Atonement is effected, not by altering the relation of God to man, but by disclosing the actual relation and attitude of the Father towards his erring children. All who now hold that our redemption is accomplished by the knowledge of God which Christ brings may claim Clement as their theological ancestor.

The doctrines in which Clement's characteristic thinking most conspicuously emerges are his teaching about God, man, punishment, and the higher or Gnostic life. In his doctrine of God Clement followed the teaching of his philosophical progenitors, Plato and Philo. And, indeed, the whole trend of belief in the second century was towards the transcendence of God. The impossibility of his holding any direct living relationship with the world was freely taught by the Gnostics. And, in opposing Gnosticism, Clement did not repudiate the idea which lay at its root, although he evaded its consequences. With him God is the Absolute, the Monad. You cannot apply to Him the terms genus, difference, species, atom, number, accident, subject, whole, part, figure; nor can any name be properly or essentially given Him. But while thus exhausting language to emphasize the remoteness and incomprehensibility of God, Clement yet believed in his immanence. All things and persons are penetrated by the Divine Logos, the Son who is the consciousness of the Father. Through the Logos God has dwelt with men, has guided and educated the race, has been, in all ages and races, anticipating the Incarnation.

The Gnostics believed in a God who was good but not just. Accordingly Clement devotes a part of his "Paidagogos" to demonstrate that goodness and justice are not incompatible. "The justice of God is good, and his goodness just." And, hence, instead of holding with the Gnostics that punishment was the work of a subordinate and evil God, Clement holds that all punishment is remedial and for the sake of the punished. In this also he followed Plato, but, as Dr. Bigg has clearly shown, unadvisedly; for, whereas Plato held that sin is the result of ignorance and is therefore a disease, Clement held that sin is the product of will. If sin is a disease, punishment may be remedial. But if sin is, as the Alexandrines held it to be, rebellion against God and against Law, the case is altered. "Punishment is the safeguard of Law, that is to say, of the unity, life, and welfare of the whole, and of the individual in and through the whole. It does not aim at amendment, but at the maintenance of that Law, which alone can amend." On Clement's theory of punishment, also, it is difficult to find the full significance of the death of Christ, or even to perceive its necessity.

In the characteristics of Clement's theology now indicated many Christians of our own time will find their prototype and legitimization, but it will be less obvious where contemporary analogies are to be found for the teaching which was most peculiar to him, his inculcation of a lower and higher grade of Christian life. No doubt we everywhere find that practically Christians are divided into those who take their Christianity seriously and those who do not, and we also find some popular forms of teaching which might be construed into a belief that there are lesser and greater mysteries into which Christians can be initiated. But in Clement we find the distinction between the ordinary believer and the Gnostic or advanced Christian elaborated and formulated. He believes the distinction to be justified by St. Paul's distinction between the babes who require to be fed with milk and the adult or spiritual who can use solid food. The Gnostic is distinguished from the common believer by many characteristics; he acts from the principle of love, the common believer from fear or hope. The perfection of the former consists in doing good, of the latter in abstinence from evil. The Gnostic prays only in thought; his excellence consists, not in controlling his desires and wishes and passions, but in not having them; in him the struggle between inclination and the sense of duty is past. The Gnostic is a king; nay, he becomes a god. His appellation of "Gnostic" is justified by Clement's theory that "knowledge is superior to faith," that "through knowledge faith is perfected, as through it alone the believer becomes perfect." "Faith is a compendious knowledge of things which are of urgent necessity; knowledge, a firm and valid demonstration of things received through faith." The final state of the Gnostic is perpetual contemplation of God. "The Gnostic soul, in the grandeur of contemplation, embraces not the divine in a mirror or through a glass, but feasts eternally upon the vision in all its clearness — that vision with which the soul, smitten with boundless love, can never be satiated — and enjoys inexhaustible gladness for endless ages, honoured by a permanent continuance in all excellence."

Here, it will be obvious, we have a strange combination of Paulinism, Gnosticism, Mysticism, and Stoicism. The relief and quickening which Stoicism brought to many of the truest souls in the Roman world proves that it does, in a large if not in a perfect measure, satisfy human instincts and cravings. Mysticism baptizes it without enforcing that element in Christianity which sanctifies work and commonplace people. That a state of absolute superiority to pleasure and pain can be reached, that this condition of "apathy" can be attained by the contemplation of God, and that this is the perfect bliss and eternal state of the soul — these are the main contentions of Mysticism. The superiority of the Gnostic to the common believer is the very point which Bossuet saw to be the foundation of all Madame Guyon's error. "The doctrines which you advance, Madame, involve the fact of an inward experience above the common experience of Christians." But anything which even seems to throw a slight on the Christianity of the uneducated and toiling millions, or of the men who spend themselves in active efforts for the promotion of Christ's kingdom, is earnestly to be deprecated. Indeed, we have a personal interest in maintaining the sufficiency of the lower Christian life; for, as Dr. Bigg appositely remarks:

"To most of us probably Miss Rossetti's words go home:

"We are of those who tremble at Thy Word,
  Who faltering walk in darkness towards our
    close
 Of mortal life, by terrors curbed and spurred —
  We are of those.

"Not ours the heart Thy loftiest love hath stirred,
  Not such as we Thy lily and Thy rose,
 Yet, Hope of those who hope with hope deferred —
  We are of those."

V

ST. AUGUSTINE AS A PROPHET

V

ST. AUGUSTINE AS A PROPHET

BY THE REV. ARTHUR C. MCGIFFERT, D.D.,

Professor of Church History in Union Theological Seminary.

EVERY true prophet looks both forward and backward — is at once parent of the future and child of the past. Only as his life draws its nourishment from the world in which he lives, with all its heritage of bygone ages, can he stamp himself upon his own generation and mould the life of generations yet to come. Not one in the world's long line of "speakers for God" whose divine message has not borne the imprint of earthly traditions and conditions — often of the organs at whose reformation or eradication that message was aimed! Indeed, the influence of every such prophet has been measured always, not alone by the divine truth which he has lived and spoken, but also by the degree to which the thought and feeling of his fellows have found utterance in him. He has spoken, not simply to his age, but for it, if he has spoken with power and effect. It should, therefore, not cause surprise if in the thinking and teaching of Augustine, who for fourteen centuries has influenced where he has not dominated the thought of Western Christendom, there should voice themselves along with his own peculiar message the prevailing tendencies of his time. It is hardly just to hold him responsible for all that he received from his age as well as for all that he gave it, and it is curiously unhistoric to overlook, as is often done, that which was truly his own, and to stamp with his name that alone which was the common property of his day and generation.

Augustine was born and bred in the midst of an environment distinctly Roman in its character, and he knew Christianity before his conversion chiefly, if not solely, in that peculiarly Latin form which it had acquired already more than a century before, and which is nowhere more clearly portrayed than in the writings of his own countrymen, the lawyer Tertullian and the ecclesiastic Cyprian. In that Christianity the most characteristic feature was the dominance of legalism. The Gospel was regarded as a law or a collection of laws, by the observance of which a man could gain eternal life, but the disregard of which entailed eternal condemnation. God was conceived commonly under the aspect of Lawgiver and Judge, whose chief function was to reward men for obeying and to punish them for disobeying his commands. Faith still had a place as the initial act of the Christian life, and God's grace was still exercised through the "sacrament of regeneration" for the remission of sins committed before baptism; but for the Christian who sinned after receiving the cleansing rite there was nothing to depend upon but his own endeavours, divided between the attempt to obey and the effort to atone by works of penance for his daily acts of disobedience. The Christian life had thus become largely a mere matter of calculation. Not the overflow of the heart in love and gratitude to God; not the instinctive striving of the soul after higher and better things for their own sake; but the payment of enough, and no more than enough, to insure escape from death and the enjoyment of the promised reward.

Naturally associated with such a conception of the Christian life was the tendency to push God ever further and further away — to lose all sense of communion with him — to regard him as a tyrant to be feared and appeased rather than as a Father to be loved. It would carry us too far afield to trace the rise and development of this conception of God in Christian thought, but the resemblance between it and the God idea in Latin paganism is striking, and the predilection for it of the native Roman mind is unmistakable.

The same legalistic tendency which operated thus to degrade the Christian life and the Christian's God resulted also in the transformation of the primitive Christian brotherhood into the Holy Catholic Church of the third and following centuries. That which had been originally a mere communion of saints, bound together by a common faith and a common hope, had become already at an early day a great and thoroughly organized institution with its apostolic episcopate and its clerical sacerdotalism — an institution claiming to be the sole representative of divine authority, rebellion against which meant rebellion against God himself, and claiming to be the sole channel of divine grace, outside whose pale salvation was impossible. It was to such a Christianity, embodied in such a Church, that Augustine was converted, under the preaching of the great Bishop Ambrose of Milan, and it is in the light of this environment that his Christian life and teaching must be studied. That he was affected by it and that much of his thinking bears its impress, that he showed himself, indeed, in his controversies with heretics and schismatics, a devout believer not only in the authority of the Church and in its right to demand implicit obedience both in thought and deed, but also in its exclusive privilege to dispense the saving grace of God, cannot be denied; and that he helped thereby to fasten upon the neck of Western Christendom the yoke of ecclesiasticism and sacramentarianism is doubtless true, but it is not this side of his teaching that is truly characteristic of him. It is not in what he received from his age, but in what he gave it, that his real significance lies. He had been no prophet had he simply voiced the thinking of his day. It was because he had another message to utter — a message received direct from God — that his name still lives beside the names of Paul and Luther.

"Thou movest us to delight in praising Thee; for Thou hast formed us for Thyself, and our heart is restless till it rests in Thee."

"I could not exist at all, O my God, unless Thou wert in me. Or should I not rather say that I could not exist unless I were in Thee, from whom are all things, by whom are all things, in whom are all things?" "O Thou strength of my soul, enter into it and prepare it for Thyself, that Thou mayst have and hold it without spot or wrinkle." "I call Thee into my soul, which, by the desire that Thou inspirest in it, Thou preparest for Thy reception." "Thou, Lord, hast blotted out all my evil deserts that Thou mightst not repay into my hands wherewith I have fallen from Thee, and Thou hast anticipated all my good deserts that Thou mightst repay into Thy hands wherewith Thou madest me." "I can do all things through Him which strengtheneth me. Strengthen Thou me that I may be able. Give what Thou commandest, and command what Thou wilt." "Another have I heard entreating that he might receive . . . by which it appeareth, O my holy God, that Thou givest when that Thou commandest to be done is done."

It is in such utterances as these, selected almost at random from his "Confessions," that the true Augustine speaks. His response to his contemporaries' low and unchristian conception of God is the abiding love of God, which leads Him to give all to man, who deserves nothing ; the constant nearness of God, which makes intimate communion with Him always a possibility ; the fatherhood of God, which makes an unbroken fellowship with Him the supreme delight of the soul. His response to his contemporaries' commercial notions of the Christian life is the allness of God and the nothingness of man ; the assertion that all that is good comes from God, and God alone ; that man is good only in so far as he depends upon God and cleaves to Him ; that no man can put God in his debt or establish a claim of merit over against Him, for there is no merit except God's merit, and to be independent of God is to be only evil. For an explanation of Augustine's thought of God and of man's relation to Him we may look in the Psalms and in the Epistles of Paul, which were his very meat and drink, and which he understood and appreciated as no one else in the ancient Church ; or we may look in Neo-Platonism, which profoundly influenced him at a critical period in his career, and which constituted for him a bridge from scepticism to the Catholic faith. With its conception of Deity as the only true existence, and of absorption in the divine as the only true good, it doubtless did much to mould his thought. But though we may acknowledge Augustine's indebtedness to these and other influences, we must recognize the fact that his theology, like his piety, finds his ultimate ground only in his profound religious nature and in his vivid experience. His was a nature to which the divine was as necessary as the air he breathed, a nature open on its upward side towards the infinities, and finding no satisfaction in aught that failed to breathe their inspiration. Even had he never known Christianity he must have sought and remained unsatisfied until he found Deity, for he was impelled Godward by the deepest craving of his soul. "Thou hast made us for Thyself, and our heart is restless till it rests in Thee," is the cry, not alone of Augustine the Christian, but of Augustine the man, and Christianity was what it was to him, not, as to so many others, because it promised him escape from punishment or the enjoyment of reward, but because it opened to him a vision of the God he had been seeking, because speaking in and through it he heard and recognized God's voice. He was the prophet, not of a distant God, but of a God within man; not of a God who has withdrawn and hidden himself from his creatures, but of a God who still reveals himself to those who will but open their eyes and look upon him. He was the prophet of such a God, and he prophesied whereof he knew. He spoke to his fellows out of the fulness of a God-knowledge gained by direct and intimate communion with Him. He bore witness to what he had himself seen in his immediate visions of the Father's face. The secret of his marvellous influence over his own and subsequent generations lies largely in this very fact, that he prophesied, not of what he had heard or thought, but of what he had experienced — that he uttered not merely his ideas, but himself. Divine truth was incorporated into his life before it found its way to his lips; he lived his theology before he taught it.

The dogma of original sin, for instance, which Augustine asserted so strenuously in his controversy with the Pelagians, and which has brought such widespread disrepute upon him, was no scholastic or artificial thing; it was in the truest sense the fruit of his own experience; nor was it out of line with his highest thought of God and man. The more vividly conscious he was of the presence of the divine, the more certain did he become of the essential kinship between God and man — a kinship which made necessary some thorough-going explanation of humanity's all-too-patent lack of present oneness with Deity, in disposition and in sympathy. His insistence upon the dogma bears witness to the strength of his conviction that man was made for God and finds his true life only in Him, and to the keenness of his experience of the empty and unsatisfying character of man's ordinary life, compared with the possibilities of a life of unbroken converse with the divine. And so the doctrine of unconditional predestination, upon which he also laid such earnest stress, rooted itself, not in any artificial conception of God and of man's relation to him, but in the experimental knowledge that God alone is good and the source of good, and that there is no such thing as independent, self-originated human merit. However harshly this truth may have found expression in the controversies in which Augustine was engaged — however narrowly and artificially it may have been interpreted at times by Augustine himself —

however unwarrantably it may have been made to justify extreme and erroneous conceptions of man and of God's dealings with him, the utterance of such a truth must have stamped Augustine as a true prophet of God in whatever age and under whatever circumstances he had spoken. The utterance of it in an age permeated with the belief that man and God have nothing in common, and that God blesses only the man whose independent, self-originated merit makes him rightfully God's creditor, stamps him as one of the very greatest of all God's prophets. His was indeed the voice of one crying in the wilderness — proclaiming to his fellows the message which Christ himself had uttered when he revealed God in human form, and thus disclosed the true source of all that is truly good in man.

Augustine has often been accused of giving currency, especially through his " Confessions," to an unhealthful mysticism which inevitably leads to quietism and saps the energy of the Christian life. There was undoubtedly an element of mysticism in Augustine's piety — as in that of all the world's great religious geniuses — but his mysticism was not that of the East, and the pantheistic mysticism which was so widespread in the West during the later Middle Ages had its progenitor not in Augustine but in the Neo-Platonism of Pseudo-Dionysius. Genuine Latin that he was, Augustine dealt in terms of personality rather than in terms of nature, and it was not of a physical union between Deity and humanity that he thought, but of a personal union between God and man. It is a fact of great significance that it was not through his study of the universe, but through his study of himself, that his eyes were at length opened to the God he had so long been seeking. "God and the soul — that is what I desire to know," he says in his Soliloquies. "Nothing more? nothing whatever."

He was a psychologist before he was a theologian, and his apprehension of his own individuality was far too vivid to permit him to content himself in genuine mystic fashion with the idea of a mere absorption in Deity as the end of existence, while his acquaintance with the inmost workings of his own soul was too thoroughgoing for him to conceive of any union between God and man which was not conditioned primarily upon a conscious unity of will and purpose. And so he found, not in mere contact of nature with nature, whether through mystic contemplation or through participation in the sacrament of the body and blood of incarnate Deity, but in the love of the human heart for God, the true secret of oneness with Him. This was the Christianity which he preached: the heart of man responding to the heart of God — love answering love — self lost, not in the contemplation of Deity, but in devotion to Him. Truly, motive power enough in such teaching to transform the life of Christendom!

Augustine did not live in vain. It is true that many of the traditional misconceptions which his higher views should have led him to repudiate find expression in his writings, and that much that is artificial and unhealthful in Christianity has in his teaching a warrant for its existence ; but, in spite of the fact that he was a child of his age and was unable to free himself completely from its bondage, he gave to those who came after him a conviction of the abiding grace of God and of man's constant dependence upon him which had in it the seeds of better things to come. This very conviction might, as it did in subsequent generations, bind the yoke of ecclesiasticism even more tightly upon the neck of Christendom by magnifying the need of that grace which the Church alone could dispense; but, in spite of the evil consequences which flowed from such a tendency, Augustine's conception of God was and remained a blessing. God a Father instead of a mere Avenger, even if the Father only of those within the Catholic Church; God near instead of far, even if near only in the sacraments: this was no small gain; and there came a time when the great truth uttered by Augustine found a clearer-eyed and surer-voiced champion in Augustine's greater disciple, Luther. Their Gospel was one, but eleven centuries of ecclesiasticism and sacramentarianism had taught the later prophet what the earlier had not learned. The evangelicism of the great Reformation of the sixteenth century was Augustine's, its Protestantism was Luther's own.

VI

JOHN WYCLIFFE

VI

JOHN WYCLIFFE

BY THE VERY REV. W. H. FREMANTLE, D.D.

WYCLIFFE was a prophet. We must not limit the spirit of prophecy to the Old Testament. Not only do we read of prophets in New Testament times at Antioch (Acts xiii. 1) and Corinth (1 Cor. xii. 28), but also in the ancient writing called the "Didache" and in the hymn "Te Deum." Why should we confine prophecy to those first Christian ages? On the tomb of Luther the inscription rightly stands, "Propheta Germaniæ."

The special character of the prophet is that of one who speaks for God; and of one who does this, not as a scribe who reads from a book, nor as an ordinary pastor who makes use of all the means at hand to influence men, but as one in direct communion with the Unseen. And, further, the prophet's message is always one of Righteousness. He disentangles God's righteousness from the wrappings of system, and makes it stand out bright and burning before the eyes of men.

But there are differences in the form which the message takes, and the medium through which it operates. Carlyle presents to us the Hero in different guises — as Priest, as Statesman, as Man of Letters. We may do the same with the Prophets. In Wycliffe we may see the Prophet as Schoolman. The Schoolmen, too, had their different titles. Aquinas was the Angelic, Bonaventura the Seraphic, Ockham the Invincible or the Singular. Wycliffe was the Evangelical Doctor. The Evangelical Righteousness which filled his soul is the key to all his thought and teaching. It led him, first, to maintain the Scriptures as supreme above traditions, Fathers, councils, Papal decrees; secondly, to uphold the rights of the nation, as the organ of public righteousness, against the Pope and the clergy; thirdly, to insist on the paramount importance of the pastoral office over the work of the monastic orders; and, lastly, to rehandle the doctrine of the Church in the light of Scripture and of sound reason. All this makes him to be justly esteemed as the pioneer, or Morning Star, of the Reformation.

Wycliffe was born about 1320, at Spresswell, near Old Richmond on the Tees, in the north of Yorkshire, close to the village of Wycliffe, from which his family took its name. But, like other prophets, he was without honour in his own house; his family were, and remained, strong Papists. Of his early training we know nothing; he probably went to Oxford about the age of fifteen, and became a scholar and afterwards a Fellow of Balliol College. This College, which had been founded by John of Balliol in 1262 and consolidated by his widow Dervorquilla in 1282, was connected with Wycliffe's country through the endowments which they had given it (and which it still possesses) at Bernard Castle on the Tees, and was the rallying-place for the "Boreales" or Northern men, as Merton College was for the Southerners.

The colleges at Oxford were at first little more than lodging-houses where poor scholars were provided for while they were reading for the higher degrees. When Wycliffe joined the University, there were, in the College which has attained in our day a leading academical and social position, twenty-two Fellows, with a weekly allowance of eight farthings apiece for maintenance ; they were bound to resign when they took the degree of Master of Arts, and their Master was elected from among themselves. Their position was improved in 1341 by the benefactions of Sir William Felton and Sir Philip Somerville, through which their allowance was increased to twelve farthings a week (equal to about five shillings now), with clothing ; six Theological Fellowships were instituted ; and the Fellows were allowed to remain till they should attain a sufficient living from the Church. Since the rule still remained that the Master must be elected from among the Fellows, it is all but certain that Wycliffe held one of these Fellowships till he was made Master, about the year 1358.

In 1361 Wycliffe was appointed Rector of Fillingham, in Norfolk ; in 1369 he changed this benefice for that of Ludgershall, in Bucks, some ten miles from Oxford ; and in 1374 he was appointed by the Crown to be Rector of Lutterworth, which position he held till his death in 1384. At the first of these parishes he seems to have seldom resided ; the leave of absence which he craved in 1368 from the Bishop of Norwich in a still extant petition, in order that he might devote himself to study at Oxford, probably denotes his usual practice, a practice common in that and many other times; at Ludgershall, as being nearer to Oxford, he was probably more constantly resident, and at Lutterworth he fully discharged the pastoral duties. His increased sense of responsibility and of the importance of the pastoral office no doubt made him unwilling to hold the cure of souls as a mere benefice. Yet he was often in Oxford, even till his last years; he appears to have had some connection with Queen's College, where his name occurs as occupying a room.

His studies began with what was called the Trivium — Grammar, Dialectics, and Rhetoric; and the Quadrivium — Arithmetic, Geometry, Astronomy, and Music. But there is evidence that he studied with enthusiasm Natural Science and Natural History; and he became thoroughly versed in legal studies, not only in the Canon and Civil Law, to which he would necessarily be led by theology and Church history, but also the laws of England. Oxford was at that time the most celebrated university in Europe. It had produced within one hundred years Roger Bacon, the physicist (the

Doctor Mirabilis, d. 1292); Grostete, the just and patriotic Bishop of Lincoln (d. 1253); Duns Scotus, the Realist (d. 1308); William of Ockham, the Nominalist (d. 1347); Richard Fitzralph, the opponent of the Mendicant Orders (Archbishop of Armagh, 1347); and Thomas Bradwardine, the Doctor Profundus, the Predestinarian (d. as Archbishop of Canterbury, 1349). Of each of these we may trace the influence in Wycliffe's writings. Yet he stands forth as entirely original. In answer to one who accuses him of taking his opinions from Ockham, he says: "My convictions owe their origin neither to him nor to me, but are irrefragably established by Holy Scripture." He was recognized by all his contemporaries at Oxford as the first man among them in knowledge and in dialectical skill. His diligence, his resource in argument, his biting wit, his wealth of illustration, all contributed to this; but, far more than all, his force of character and deep conviction, his genuine and humble piety, and his entire reliance on the Scriptures. He is never the mere apologist or argumentative fencer, but a preacher of righteousness. In his last complaint to the Parliament (1382) he does not take up a position of self-defence, but boldly demands that, in spite of Pope and bishops, free course should be allowed to the preaching of the true doctrine of the Sacraments.

The time was one of great unsettlement, such as needs a strong man. The English nation was all on fire with the long war with France, at one moment drunk with prosperity, at another dejected by the loss of all its greatness; the Black Death (1348) stalked across Europe and mowed down half the inhabitants of England, producing the usual results of pestilence — panic, recklessness, a dislocation of human relations, and begetting wild hopes by the sudden rise of wages and of prices through the paucity of labourers. The system of the Middle Ages was coming to an end; the Popes had left Rome for Avignon (1305), and their return to Rome in 1376 produced the great schism which shook men's allegiance. Intellectually, also, the world was changing. Scholasticism was waning, the Renaissance was dawning with Petrarch and Boccaccio. And there was an uprising of the common people, not merely to get rid of serfdom, as under Wat Tyler and John Ball in 1381, but to gain knowledge, as is witnessed by the poem of "Piers Plowman," in which Truth reveals herself, not to the lord or the ecclesiastic, but to the peasant. Till this time Latin had been the language of the scholar, the divine, and the lawyer, as French had been that of the court; but now Wycliffe in his Bible and his later works, Langland in his popular poem, and the courtly Chaucer in his Tales, laid the foundations of English literature. This in Wycliffe's case was not so much a literary change as an appeal to the popular heart, grounded on the noble belief that simple men are capable of developing the highest powers: "One simple man," he says, "if the grace of Christ be in him, is more profitable to the Church than many graduates, since he sows Christ's law humbly and abundantly by work as well as by word."

The change just noticed, the appeal of the scholastic divine to the people, is a genuine product of Christian thought. The Schoolmen had many authorities to which they appealed with equal confidence — the Scriptures, the Fathers, Aristotle, the decrees of Popes and Councils. Gradually but surely Wycliffe raises the Scriptures above the rest, and places them on a pedestal where their unique value is perceived. And, as time goes on, and he is met by obduracy on the part of those in high place, he is convinced that it is not learning but spiritual enlightenment which enables men to apprehend truth, and he turns to the people; the Scriptures must be given to them in their own tongue, and must be set forth by plain men in plain words. "If you mix too many flowers with the seed," he says, "it will not take root." This led first to the formation of his own philosophical views on a directly Scriptural basis, and valuing the simple teaching of Christ and the Apostles above all the subtleties of the schools; then to the translation of the Bible into English, then to the writing of English sermons and tracts, and to the training of a body of Poor Priests, who, like the Franciscans in a former and the Wesleyans in a later century, went to and fro among the people, bringing the simple elements of divine truth into their hearts and their homes.

The righteousness of which Wycliffe was the prophet had to be carried into public life; he became a legist and a statesman. It is probable that he sat in Parliament, not only in the "Good Parliament" of 1376, when the Black Prince rose from his death-bed to aid the cause of moral reform in court and council, but also in 1366, when the question of tribute paid to the Pope was discussed with great vehemence. It is known that six Masters of Arts were summoned by the King to that Parliament, and that Wycliffe speaks of himself as " the King's own clerk "; that he gives a long account of the speeches of seven Lords in the debate; and that he reports certain words of the Bishop of Rochester as addressed to him "in the public sitting of Parliament." The tribute of 1000 marks a year had been imposed on King John by Innocent III. as the price of the restoration of the kingdom and the acknowledgment that the Pope was overlord of England. It had never been paid willingly, and for thirty-three years had not been paid at all; the Pope demanded payment with arrears. And this claim was connected with the numerous exactions of the Papacy, such as that of the first year's income of all benefices. Arnald, the Pope's treasurer, had an office in London, at which these dues or exactions were paid. In the process of the dispute, which lasted many years, it was shown that the Pope (and a French Pope living at Avignon) habitually appointed to English church offices favourites of his own who never set foot in the realm, and that the revenues going out of England to the Pope were four times as large as those paid to the King. Wycliffe wrote a tract on the oath of Arnald, taken on his appointment, in which he swore that he would do nothing contrary to the interests of the realm, that he would give good advice to the King, and that he would conform to the laws of England. In every particular, as Wycliffe shows, this oath had been violated; the pecuniary interests of the Pope had been made to override all law and justice. The clergy stood by the Pope; but the laity were grateful to a theologian who could vindicate the cause of England against the rapacity of foreigners which was cloaked with holy sanctions. The court and the people stood by him, with hardly an exception, to the end.

It was not as a partisan that Wycliffe took this course, but from a profound sense of justice. Righteousness was more to him than clerical interests. And this led him further. He was sent on an embassy to Bruges in 1374 to treat with the envoys of the Pope on the questions just mentioned; and at the same time an embassy under John of Gaunt, Duke of Lancaster, was sent to Bruges to make peace with France. Both embassies proved futile; but the occasion had three important consequences for Wycliffe. First, it made him more fully acquainted with the duplicity of the Pope and of the English clergy who were under his influence; secondly, it commended him to Lancaster, who ever afterwards stood by him; and, thirdly, it placed him on an eminence as a patriot when the refusal of the Pope to do justice was debated next year in Parliament.

But Wycliffe was led much further. He saw that the clergy must be brought under the national law. He maintained that the nation had the right, not merely of taxing them (for hitherto they had been exempt), but of depriving them of their estates if this were expedient for the good of the country and of religion. And he came more and more to the conviction that the possession of land, with the feudal position which it implied, was prejudicial to both Church and realm. He even wrote to the Pope exhorting him to disembarrass himself of his temporal sovereignty as an example to the clergy throughout Christendom. The requirements and laws of the country, not the hierarchical position of the clergy, must regulate public policy if righteousness was to prevail.

To these victories he gave systematic expression in his great work "De Dominio." God is the righteous ruler to whom all sovereignty belongs, but he has given parts of it, as a stewardship, to those who rule under Him, to the Pope and clergy, to the king and magistrates, and to each believer according to his position. Each of these, as holding under Him (for the feudal idea is still dominant), so far as he is faithful to the great Overlord, is supreme in his own sphere. Thus, in contradistinction to the Papal theory (constantly set forth by the image of the plurality of the keys or the two swords in Peter's hands) that the Pope is supreme over all departments of life, Wycliffe asserts the sacredness of the human conscience and human relations in themselves, and their immunity from Papal interference. His more popular tract " On the Six Yokes " — that is, the social relations which are binding on us all — is an anticipation of William Tyndale's " Obedience of a Christian Man." The clergy are to minister faithfully and in subordination to the Scriptures, their faithfulness being judged of by the nation to which they minister; that is their sphere; but in all other spheres the ruler, be he king or father or master, or simple individual, is responsible to God alone. The natural law of human society is the law of God's righteousness.

This sense of the need of righteousness in all departments of life led Wycliffe, in the next place, to recognize the paramount value of the pastoral office above all parts of the Church system. It led him in his old age to leave the University, its philosophy and its disputations, the scenes of his intellectual triumphs, for a country parish; to esteem the effort to raise the common life by pastoral intercourse of more importance than the solitary and unearthly piety aimed at in monasteries and colleges, and to bend all his energies to the translation of the Bible, the issuing of plain English tracts and sermons, and the training of his Poor Priests.

We may best view the country parson of those days through the description of him given by Chaucer, who is supposed to have had Wycliffe as the model for his picture: "He was a learned man, a clerk, . . . preaching Christ's Gospel truely, wondrous diligent, patient in times of adversity, willing to give rather than exact from his flock."

Wide was his parish, and houses far asunder,
But he ne left nought ne for rain nor thunder,
In sickness and in mischief, to visit
The farthest in his parish, much and lit,
Upon his feet, and in his hand a staff.
This noble example to his sheep he yaf [gave],
That he first wrought, and afterwards he taught.

This description certainly appears to fall in with the views of the pastoral office which Wycliffe entertained. The parochial life differs from the monastic in that it brings the pastor in contact with the common experience of men and all its varied discipline. It differs also from the life of the evangelist or revival preacher in that it does not touch men merely at one point, but enters into their homes and their business; and it would seem that Wycliffe, like Fitzralph of Armagh, contrasted the life of the parson or "secular" priest with that of the friars on this ground as well as on the ground of their having become corrupt and self-seeking, and of their being the special emissaries of the Pope. It is certain that in his later life he regarded them as a power which did not make for righteousness; so much so that on one occasion, when he was ill, he suddenly roused himself, exclaiming, "I shall not die, but live and declare the works of the Friars." He would have wished the parochial clergy to be married, so that they might be more closely in contact with the life of the people. And we may connect this zeal for parochial well-being with his public spirit and desire for righteousness in the nation; for the parish is a fraction of the nation.

The great instrument for his parochial work and teaching was the English Bible, at which he laboured on, revising and correcting, to the end of his life. The translation was made from the Latin Vulgate, for both Greek and Hebrew were then inaccessible. Wycliffe was assisted by his friends Nicholas Hereford and John Purvey, the latter of whom revised the whole after the Master's death. To this were added many simple tracts and short sermons in English (almost all the English works belong to this time of his life) which served as guides to his itinerant preachers.

It would appear that Wycliffe had during his Oxford days gathered round him a few scholars whom he trained as preachers. Their numbers were now largely added to. They were mostly very simple men, like the first Franciscans or the first Methodists. Wycliffe applies to them the word "Idiotes," which was given to the Apostles by the Sanhedrin. They went about clad in a long russet gown, preaching and singing in a way which earned them the name of Lollards (babblers or chaunters), appealing as men of the people to their own order, and endeavouring in their rude way to free religion, especially the sacrament, from its superstitious elements, and to waken men up to righteousness and "the law of Christ," as Wycliffe constantly called the simple Christianity which he delighted to teach.

But little or nothing would have been done had Wycliffe's reform not touched the errors of doctrine which were stifling the Gospel. His glory is that he attempted to shake the whole fabric of Papal error. He judged the whole by its bearing on righteousness. The Pope, so Wycliffe taught, is to be resisted when acting unrighteously; the support and allegiance of the faithful is to be withdrawn from the clergy when they are untrue to their calling. The Church is not a body of persons conforming to certain ordinances of which the clergy hold the key, but the entire body of the elect. The moral and independent standing which election implies is all in all. The sacrament is the receiving of Christ by means of the sign or emblem; and the change wrought in the elements is that they become capable of bringing home the person or presence of Christ to the believing heart. This, at least, seems to be the meaning of Wycliffe's expressions, which are couched in scholastic forms. Transubstantiation, on the other hand, he utterly rejects. How can the "accidents" of taste or touch remain if the substance is changed? A shrew-mouse would detect the fallacy. In the great matter of justification Wycliffe does not take the same ground as Luther; not that he differs from him, but that the aspect of the Gospel which he chiefly realizes is not that of conferring the pardon of sin, but that of leading men into living participation in the divine righteousness. He views the whole process of redemption through the medium of God's sovereignty, and dwells on the election of men to righteousness, though not overriding free will and not admitting the idea of reprobation.

We may see now the way in which Wycliffe was a precursor of the Reformation. He was a prophet nourishing his soul directly from the source of eternal life, not through the media of human inventions, and speaking directly for God and for righteousness. This is indeed the essence of the Reformation doctrine, that we are righteous through faith alone; for what is meant by faith is not some formal belief, or acceptance of some special truth, but the spiritual enlightenment, the expression of the divine life in the soul, that which "makes evident the things not seen," and "endures as seeing Him who is invisible." This faith Wycliffe possessed in the highest degree. It was this which made him realize the supremacy of Scripture above all writings, and of Christ above all human things, "our only Emperor, Lord, Bishop, and Abbot." It was this which made him assert the divine sovereignty, with which no human will or invention can conflict. It was this which made him take an independent attitude towards church ordinances, and use them only as conducive to righteousness, but which also gave so high a value in his eyes to plain preaching and the manifestation of truth to the conscience. It was this, finally, which made him assert the independent validity of the gifts or ministries assigned to each believer, and, as a corollary from this, the divine functions of human government — an assertion which was renewed by the reformers of the sixteenth century only to be buried again beneath a heap of scholastic disputations; an assertion, nevertheless, which needs as much now as in his day to be renewed and made practical if Christianity is ever to master the world.

The meed accorded to Wycliffe was that which the world has usually accorded to the prophets. He was arraigned as a heretic by Courtenay, first as Bishop of London, in 1377, before the Convocation at St. Paul's, when he was saved by the appearance at his side of John of Gaunt, who quarrelled violently with the Bishop and prevented any action being taken; and again by the same prelate as Archbishop of Canterbury, at Lambeth, in 1382, when he was saved by the intervention of the Queen Mother, the widow of the Black Prince, and by the threatening attitude of the citizens of London, who honoured him. His University was forced by the Pope and the Archbishop to condemn various propositions from his writings, but he, being present, manfully defended himself; and no one dared either to touch his person or to subject him to excommunication. His advice was sought by the King on his relations with the Pope at the very time when the ecclesiastical power was trying to destroy him; and he continued his work at Lutterworth unimpeded, and, though touched with paralysis in 1383, displayed an astonishing activity in pastoral and literary labours to the end. At length, on the last day of 1384, he was struck down by a second paralytic seizure, during the sacrament, and died with his friends around him.

His body was exhumed in 1428 in pursuance of a decree of the Council of Constance, and his ashes thrown into the Swift. But meanwhile his works had been carried far and wide. In Bohemia, which they reached through those about Anne of Bohemia, wife of Richard II., they inspired new prophets, Hus and Jerome of Prague, who were treacherously put to death for propagating his opinions by the Council of Constance, and gave rise to a national movement which, though quenched in bloodshed, leavened the life of the whole people. In England it was said at the beginning of the fifteenth century that every third man was a Lollard; and the first Parliament of Henry V. was so swayed by Wycliffe's anticlerical principles that the ecclesiastics trembled for their estates. But the renewal of the

French wars drew the whole mind of the country in another direction; and the movement of Wycliffe, already compromised during his lifetime by its supposed connection with Wat Tyler's agrarian revolt, was finally discredited when its leader, Sir John Oldcastle, was provoked in 1417 to take arms against his King. But though Lollardry was crushed, the influence of Wycliffe was never extinguished. As many as a hundred and fifty copies of Wycliffe's Bible still remain; and there is no doubt that it was widely read by the common people, for whom it was written, throughout the fifteenth century. When, in 1510, a raid against heretics was made by Fitzjames, Bishop of London, so violent that Colet wrote to Erasmus that all the prisons were full of them, the articles in almost all cases stated that the accused possessed copies of Wycliffe's Bible or of some of his works; and Erasmus, in his account of his pilgrimage to the shrine of Becket, at Canterbury, when he tells how his companion (Colet) questioned the advantage of such an exhibition of relics, represents his interlocutor as saying: "Who was your friend? Some Wycliffite, I suppose." Thus the reformer of the fourteenth century joins hands with the reformer of the sixteenth.

And thus it is ever with the prophet. "In the sight of the unwise he seems to die," but "his hope is full of immortality"; his spirit lives on and prepares men for the better day.

VII

MARTIN LUTHER, THE PROPHET OF THE REFORMATION

VII

MARTIN LUTHER, THE PROPHET OF THE REFORMATION

BY PROFESSOR ADOLF HARNACK

He came in the fulness of time — when the rule of the Roman Church, which had hitherto educated the peoples, had become a tyranny, when States and nations were beginning to throw off an ecclesiastical yoke and independently to organize themselves in accordance with their own laws.

He came in the fulness of time — when the economic conditions of Europe, both through inner developments and through the discovery of distant lands, had become completely changed, and the method of administration of their estates by the Roman priests and monks was no longer tenable.

He came in the fulness of time — when mediæval churchly science had outlived its usefulness and when the tree of knowledge was producing young, fresh shoots.

He came in the fulness of time — when the classes and castes of the Middle Ages were disintegrating, and when everywhere the individual, supported by the new culture of the Renaissance, was striving to struggle up to independence. He came when the monastic idea of life had run through all phases of its development, and when man was beginning to esteem an active not less than an ascetic life.

He came in the fulness of time — when laymen were no longer satisfied with priest and sacrament, but were seeking God himself, and were feeling the personal responsibility of their own souls. He came as man was recognizing the precepts of the Church to be but arbitrary laws, and her traditions as only innovations and forgeries.

He was no universal genius, no Plato, no Leibnitz. He did not grasp all the conditions of his time; nay, he did not even know them all. His education was mediocre. He was no sharp and refined thinker, he was no humanist, he was no critic; his vocation was not to rectify theoretical errors just because they were errors. The sphere of science was not his sphere; indeed, he had an instinctive and never entirely conquered suspicion of "reason."

He was no saint, no Francis, who, through the glow of feeling, through the sweetness of his spirit or the power of his sacrifice, swept every one along with him. He was also no agitator, no orator, who, like Savonarola, could move and inflame the masses.

Luther was no cosmopolitan, but a German with the marked characteristics of his nation, a German as monk, as professor, and as reformer. His personality has never been understood by the Romanic races; it has never impressed them; his thoughts alone have been able to take root among them.

How was this man, then, able to become the reformer of the Western Church? How was it that this professor in a little German university, in the midst of an uncultivated environment, could unfetter the great movement by which the new epoch in the history of the world began? How did it happen that, through him, "the time was fulfilled"? He was in only one thing great and mighty, overwhelmingly and irresistibly the master of his time, victoriously overcoming the history of a thousand years in order to force his age into new channels. *He was great only in the rediscovered knowledge of God in the Gospels.* What it means to have a God, what this God is, how he grasps us, and how we can apprehend and hold him — all that he experienced and that he proclaimed. In the midst of the night of his conventual life, as he strove to work out his salvation in fear and trembling, it dawned upon him like the sun : " The just shall live *by faith*." In the midst of the complex system of what was called " religion," in the midst of unsatisfying consolations and of incomplete penances, he lived *religion itself*, and he led it out into freedom. The living God — not a philosophical or mystic abstraction — the manifest and gracious God, was a God to be reached by every Christian. Unchangeable reliance of the heart upon God, personal confidence of belief in Him who said, " I am thy salvation," that was to Luther the whole sum of religion. Beyond all care and trouble, beyond all arts of the ascetic, beyond all theological precepts, he dared to grasp God himself, and in this deed of faith his whole life won its independent sturdiness. " Mit unser Macht ist Nichts gethan" (" With our might is nothing done"). He knew the might which gives to our lives both firmness and freedom ; he knew that might, and he called it by its name, Belief.

To him that meant no longer an obedient acceptance of ecclesiastical dogmas, it meant no knowledge, no deed, but simply the personal and continual giving of the heart to God, a daily regeneration of man. That was his confession of faith, a living, busy, active thing, a sure trust, making one joyful and eager in the sight of God and man, something which makes us always ready to serve or to suffer. Despite all evil, yes, despite our sin and guilt, our life is hid in God, when we trust him as children trust their father. That was the vital thought and the vital power of Luther's life.

With equal certainty he perceived and experienced the other idea, the idea of "the freedom of a Christian." This freedom was to him no empty emancipation or the license for every whim. Freedom meant to Luther the liberation from every external or human authority in matters of belief and conscience. Christian freedom was to him the feeling of surety that, united with God, he was raised above the world, sin, death, and the devil. "If God be for us, who can be against us?" Every soul that has found God, and in him has recognized its refuge, is free — so proclaimed Luther.

> Ein' feste Burg ist unser Gott,
> Ein' gute Wehr und waffen.
>
> (A mighty fortress is our God,
> A bulwark never failing.)

Let it be here remarked that, in the same hymn, Luther asks:

> Fragst du, wer er ist?
> Er heisset Jesus Christ,
> Der Herr Zebaoth,
> Und ist kein and'rer Gott.
>
> (Dost ask who that may be?
> Christ Jesus, it is he,
> His name, Lord Sabaoth;
> Nor is there other God.)

In Jesus Christ alone Luther recognized God. Outside of Christ he saw only a dark, frightful, and enigmatical Force. In Christ alone he saw the gracious God. Luther was no philosopher who would recognize God in the construction of the world; he was no mystic, who could raise God out of his own soul's secret depths. He was a faithful son of the Christian Church, convinced that she was in the right with her commission from Jesus

Christ. He was a faithful disciple of Paul, and had learned from him that all knowledge of God lies locked up in the sentence, "God is the father of our Lord Jesus Christ." He was a faithful disciple of Christ himself, who said, "No man knoweth the Father save only the Son, and him to whom the Son will reveal Him."

Not only did Luther win God-knowledge in Jesus Christ, "the mirror of God's paternal heart," but also the fact that Jesus is the Redeemer, who through death has freed us from sin and blame. Paul's Gospel is also Luther's. Before the latter, no one in the Church really understood the Epistles to the Romans and to the Galatians. Just because he was convinced that he was putting the old, dimmed Gospel again in the light, he was far from the thought of adding anything to it. Never had he another plan than that *of restoring the old belief;* never did he think to fight against the Church, but always *for the Church* against a false and soul-dangerous practice ; never did he dream that the Gospel had been really lost — no, but it was to be freed from a captivity into which the Pope, the priests, and the theologians had led it.

Great, lasting reformations are made only by conservative men; not those who "destroy," but those who "fulfil," bring about a new era. Luther — at the bottom of his heart the most conservative of men — has broken the mediæval Catholic system in pieces for millions of souls, and thus freed the history of progressive humanity from the shackles of that system. In that he vindicated the new and yet old Gospel, in that he freed the conscience of the individual from priest and statute, he struck deadly blows against the Church of the Middle Ages. For, (1) he overturned her teaching as to salvation — salvation not being a thing brought about by donations and merits, but the free grace of God, which gives us the conviction that we are his children. (2) He overturned the teaching as to Christian perfection — true Christian life does not consist in monasticism, but in an active life of fidelity to a calling, in humility, patience, and the service of love to our neighbour. (3) He overturned the teachings as regards the sacrament — God does not give us individual and different fragments of grace, but he gives us the forgiveness of sins and with it all grace, yes, he gives us himself as the Bread of our lives. (4) He overturned the priestly Church-system — God wills that all his children shall be priests, and he has instituted but one office, the office of proclaiming the Gospel and of distributing forgiveness. (5) Luther overturned the mediæval church services — God will not be honoured by means of ceremonies, masses, oblations, etc., but only through praise and thanksgiving, pleading and prayer. Every church service must be spiritual, and at the same time innately bound with service to one's neighbour. (6) He overturned the false authorities of Roman Catholicism. Not the Pope, nor the Councils, not even the letter of the Bible (yet here, in regard to the Bible, Luther was himself not completely clear), has unerring authority, but only the Gospel, the power and truth of which the soul inwardly knows.

All these points have to do with religion alone. Luther determined to purify religion and to free it from every strange thing which does not belong to it. Besides this he never had another independent interest; he did not care about bettering the world, or the State, or science, for themselves alone. Yet right here is revealed the truth of the saying: "Seek ye first the kingdom of God and his righteousness, and all these things shall be added unto you." In that Luther thought out the Gospel in all its parts, proclaimed and applied it, all else fell into his lap; in that he liberated religion from mixture with that which is foreign to it, *he also liberated the natural life and the natural order of things.* He put everything in its right place, and gave everything freedom and room for development. Everywhere he broke apart unnatural ties, he loosed old chains, he gave air and light.

Theology through him is henceforth to be nothing else than the exposition of the Gospel, of how it has founded the Christian community and still keeps it together. The proof of theology is no longer derived from external authority or strange philosophical speculations, but by the simple fact of Christ's appearance, and by our inward experience.

Philosophy is no longer a feared servant or a seductive mistress of theology, but her independent sister. Languages and history are studied conscientiously and faithfully, in order to ascertain the right meaning of every word.

The State is no longer regarded as a half-sinful product of compulsion and need, and the creature of the Church, but as the God-willed, independent order of public social life.

Law does not longer pass as a dangerous middle course, something between the might of the stronger and the virtue of the Christian, but as the independent, God-given rule of intercourse, always maintained by the "powers that be."

Marriage is no longer thought of as a divine concession towards the weak, but as a free bond between the sexes, a bond instituted by God, and free from tutelage on the part of the Church, and as the school of the highest morality.

General benefactions, such as the care of the poor, are not now so much pursued because of any desire to assure one's own salvation; they have become a free service to one's neighbour, the final scope and only reward of which is effective relief.

Above all things, however, in civil (as opposed to ecclesiastical) callings, activity in house and farm, in trade and official position, is no longer looked upon suspiciously as if it led away from our spiritual vocation. Men now know that the one who guides a household well, educates children patiently and faithfully, fulfils the duties of a calling — even though that one be but a poor boy or a lowly maid — stands in the rightful spiritual place and is higher than all monks and nuns.

Over the great period which we call the Middle Ages, over the chaos of non-independent and intricate forms, there soared the spirit of belief, which had recognized its own nature and therefore had also recognized its limits. Under its sway, all things that had a right to free existence now strove towards independent development. Before Luther, no one had ever separated so clearly and distinguishingly the great departments of life, and given to each its own right. Wonderful! this man would not teach the world other than what the being, the power, and the comfort of the Christian religion is; but in that he recognized this most important department in its own individuality, all other departments came to their own. Luther preached that the just man lives by faith, and that a child of God is a free master over all things. In that he so taught he indeed freed men and things, and thus showed that "the time was fulfilled," for he was called that the time should be fulfilled.

He became *the* reformer. Beside him Zwingli

and Calvin can claim but second places; they are dependent on him. Yes, we can even say: *He was the Reformation.* He had experienced the Reformation in his own soul, when he struggled in the cloister with the creed of his Church. Everything which he afterwards said, wrote, and did, in Wittenberg, in Worms, and in Coburg, was only the natural consequence of that experience. Out of his breast, from the bottom of his heart, the Reformation streamed as a brook out of hidden springs in the rock. In one sense he did not give power and endurance to the Reformation: he did not set its bounds and aim, but the Reformation gushed from his spirit like a fruitful stream. "Here I stand; I can do no other," said he, before Emperor and Empire. When the lonely man thus spoke, it was decided that he, through his faith, like Abraham, should become the father of many thousands; it was decided that a great epoch in the history of mankind had finished its course, and a new was advancing.

But we must not forget that it was four hundred years ago that Luther taught. The convenient belief that he thought out everything for us, and that we can rest on his teaching, is a foolish one. The greatest hero is always only a *finisher* for the past; as regards the future he is but a *beginner*. He who does not understand Luther so that he learns from him the spirit with which to solve new problems and lessons, and so that he endeavours to continue the Reformer's work, understands him falsely. The prophets have been given to us, not that we should build their graves, but that we should inflame our hearts through their faith and their courage.

VIII

JOHN WESLEY

VIII

JOHN WESLEY

BY THE VERY REV. F. W. FARRAR, D.D.

IT has often happened that the most memorable revolutions or reawakenments in the moral and spiritual world have been achieved by men who were not remarkable either for learning or for genius. St. Francis of Assisi awoke the Church of the thirteenth century from its gorgeous dreams of dominion and luxury, and has eternized his name on the bright lists of sainthood; but the humble brown figure of the poor illiterate wanderer looks absolutely insignificant beside the purpureal stateliness of Pope Innocent III. There was something almost bourgeois in the plain homeliness of St. Vincent de Paul, yet in founding his sisterhoods of mercy he inaugurated the chief movements of social philanthropy. Thomas Clarkson and John Howard were simple country squires, with no remarkable endowments of any kind except the genius of goodness and the sensibility of compassion, yet the one ended the slave trade and emancipated the slave, and the other—traversing Europe, as Edmund Burke said, "to dive into the depths of dungeons, to plunge into the infection of hospitals, to take the gauge and dimensions of misery, depression, and contempt"—purified the prisons of the Christian world from their enormous abuses and dehumanized loathliness. There were many noblemen of the last generation who towered over the late Earl of Shaftesbury in the splendour of their attainments and their oratory, yet none of them, not one of the Archbishops, Bishops, and great ecclesiastics of his day, effected one tithe of his mighty work of beneficence for the poor women of the mines and collieries, for the factory children, for the little "climbing boys," for the waifs and strays and gutter-children of London, for the costermongers, for maltreated lunatics, and for hosts of the oppressed. To this order of men, though he was superior to them in learning, belonged John Wesley. He found a Church forgetful and neglectful of its duties, somnolent in the plethora of riches, and either unmindful or unwisely mindful of the poor. He found churches empty, dirty, neglected, crumbling into hideous disrepair; he found the work of the ministry performed in a manner scandalously perfunctory; he found in the ranks of the priesthood more than enow

> of such as, for their bellies' sake,
> Creep, and intrude, and climb into the fold.
> * * * * * * *
> And, when they list, their lean and flashy songs
> Grate on their scrannel pipes of wretched straw;
> The hungry sheep look up, and are not fed,
> But, swoln with wind and the rank mist they draw,
> Rot inwardly, and foul contagion spread;
> Besides what the grim wolf, with privy paw,
> Daily devours apace, and nothing said.

Doubtless in his day, as in Milton's, it might have been said,

> But that two-handed engine at the door
> Stands ready to smite once, and smite no more.

But John Wesley, becoming magnetic with moral sincerity, flashed into myriads of hearts fat as brawn, cold as ice, hard as the nether millstone, the burning spark of his own intense convictions, and thus he saved the Church, which at first had nothing for him but sneers, hatred, and persecution. Wesley never was an enemy to the Church of England. He loved the Church which hated him. He included her name in his daily "grace before meat." He died in her full communion. He would have said, as sincerely as Edmund Burke, "I wish to see the Church of England great and powerful; I wish to see her foundation laid low and deep; I would have her open wide her hospitable gates by a liberal comprehension; I would have her a common blessing to the world, an example, if not an instructor, to those who have not the happiness to belong to her; I would have her give a lesson of peace to mankind, that a vexed and wandering generation may be taught to seek refuge and toleration in the bosom of her maternal charity." And he distinctly saved the Church of England from the Nemesis of just retribution, which but for him would sooner or later have overwhelmed her in indiscriminate collapse, and might not improbably have buried under her heaps of ruin all that was best in the great heritage of English religion. He set her the example of indefatigable activity, of immense and ungrudging self-sacrifice, of that true beauty of holiness which shines in the life of every Christian who "makes his moral being his prime care," and gives the actual, not the merely nominal, sovereignty to the beliefs which he professes to regard as supreme. He saved the Church of England, though at first she so angrily and contemptuously rejected him, and, just as from the mouth of Socrates issued forth

Mellifluous streams which watered all the schools
Of Academics old and new, with those
Surnamed Peripatetics, and the sect
Epicurean, and the Stoic severe,

so, from the impulse which Wesley gave, originated almost every form of special religious enthusiasm since his day. Thus he became one of the most disinterested of those benefactors of mankind who "have raised strong arms to bring heaven a little nearer to our earth."

One great virtue in his character was that sovereign religious tolerance which is so infinitely rare amid the divergences of religious shibboleths. In the first century the heathen said, "See how these Christians love one another"; but, long before the third century, the *odium theologicum* had culminated in those execrable forms of religious virulence which, if "love" be indeed the fulfilling of the law, are the very antithesis of the Christlike spirit, at which all *profess* to aim who take Christ for an ensample that they should walk in his steps. It is a splendid testimony to Wesley's moral insight and spiritual greatness that "no reformer the world has ever seen so united faithfulness to the essential doctrines of Revelation with charity towards men of every Church and creed." This spirit of John Wesley has been found, theoretically at least, only in the best and greatest Christians.

Bishop Sanderson pointed out to some of the narrowest of the post-Reformation sectaries that "the Church was not to be confined to the narrow pingle of a room in Amsterdam." William Penn uttered the great sentiment, so dear to the heart of Abraham Lincoln, that the meek, the just, the pious, the devout, are everywhere of one religion, and that when death hath taken off these masks they will know and love one another. The devout Dominican Henri Feyrrane saw, as Lacordaire also saw, that the worst possible policy is "to make the gate of the Church bristle with anathemas, as with razors and pitchforks." But too many nominal Christians have forgotten that all these words and actions tend to reduce the Church to the same deplorable chaos of mutual hatreds and fierce disdain which Christ found among the Pharisees and Sadducees of Jerusalem, when he chose the hated and heretical Samaritan as his exemplary type of the goodness which loved its neighbour.

I dwell on this high virtue of Wesley because it is so exceptional, and because it was never more needed than in these days. Writing in advanced age to the Bishop of Lincoln, he said: "Alas! my Lord, is this a time to persecute any man for conscience' sake? I beseech you do as you would be done to. You are a man of sense; you are a man of learning; nay, I verily believe (what is of infinitely more value) you are a man of piety. Then think and let think." Again, how wise are the remarks in the preface to his Sermons: "Some may say I have mistaken the way myself, though I have undertaken to teach others. It is very possible that I have. But I trust, whereinsoever I have been mistaken, my mind is open to conviction. I sincerely desire to be better informed. What I know not, teach thou me. '*Da mihi scire*,' as says St. Augustine, '*quod sciendum est.*' If I linger in the path I have been accustomed to tread, . . . take me by the hand and lead me. . . . But be not discouraged if I ask you not to beat me down in order to quicken my pace. May I request you further not to give me hard names in order to bring me into the right way? . . . For God's sake, if it be possible, let us not provoke one another to wrath. Let us not kindle in each other this fire of hell. If we could discern truth by that dreadful light, would it not be loss rather than gain? For how far is love, even with many wrong opinions, to be preferred before truth itself without love! We may die without the knowledge of many truths, and yet be carried into Abraham's bosom. But if we die without love, what will knowledge avail? Just as much as it avails the devil and his angels!"

The ground for this wise and noble tolerance, which is one of Wesley's special lessons to this religiously distracted age, was his clear realization of the truth — demonstrated by all history — that while unity of spirit is attainable, uniformity of organization is not; that while there can be but one flock of the Good Shepherd, there always have been and to the end of time there will be many folds. Dean Stanley delighted in a story — I know not its source and will not vouch for its authenticity — which he called "Wesley's Dream." It told how Wesley dreamt that, wandering to the gate of Gehenna, he asked whether there were any Romanists, any Anglicans, any Baptists, any Calvinists, any Independents there, and was told in each case, "Yes, a great many," and was yet more deeply pained when, asking, "And are there any Wesleyans here?" it was still answered, "Yes, a great many." Then, returning to the gate of Heaven, he asked, "Are there any Romanists here?" "None whatever." "Any Anglicans?" "None whatever." "Any Baptists?" "None whatever." "Any Calvinists?" "None whatever." "Any Wesleyans?" Still none whatever. "Whom then have you here?" he asked in amazement. "We have none but Christians here," was the answer; "we know no other name." Whether the story was a pleasing allegory of the Dean's or not, I cannot tell; but this I know, that Wesley's sermon on the Catholic Spirit would have the honour of being thought shockingly lax by bigots of every denomination, yet all true Christians might well say with him, "I desire to have a league, offensive and defensive, with every soldier of Christ. We have all not only one Lord, one faith, one baptism, but we are all also engaged in one warfare."

As another of Wesley's exemplary qualities I would single out his sovereign common sense, which is also an endowment much liable to overthrow by the violences of egotistical dogmatism. Though many have identified his teaching mainly with certain formulæ, Wesley had no faith in the bare reiteration of shibboleths. His idea of a "Gospel sermon" was not the narrowly ignorant one which supposes it to consist in the incessant repetition of phrases — phrases often originally meaningless to many of those who used them, or which have become stereotyped into mere inanity and fetichism. In his diary for November 20, 1785, he writes: "I preached in Bethnal Green, and spoke as plainly as I possibly could, on having a form of godliness but denying the power thereof. And this I judged far more suitable to such a congregation than talking about justification by faith." How free, again, from all hysteric excitability was the entire attitude of his religion! Some one had been talking in an exaggerated and fantastic way about death, and asking what he would do if he knew that he would die the next day. "What should I do?" he said. "Exactly what I shall do now. I should call and talk to Mr. So-and-so, and Mrs. So-and-so; and dine at such an hour, and preach in the evening, and have supper, and then I should go to bed and sleep as soundly as ever I did in my life." His feeling about death was that, so far from being terrible, it was man's great birthright; and he would say, with the poet:

To you the thought of death is terrible,
Having such hold on life; to me it is not;
No more than is the lifting of a latch,
Or as a step into the open air
Out of a tent already luminous
With light that shines through its transparent folds.

Again, it was no small matter that, in an age so corrupt and decadent as his, in which the dregs of sensuality and worldliness poured over the glorious England of Puritanism by the despicable epoch of the Restoration had reduced religion to a Dead Sea of torpid unreality, Wesley, like the great Hebrew prophets of old, should have stood forth as a preacher of righteousness. No preacher or reformer can effect great results unless he insists upon

Christ's plain teaching that, if we would ever enter into the kingdom of heaven, we must keep the commandments. Late in his career he said: "Near fifty years ago a great and good man, Dr. Potter, then Archbishop of Canterbury, gave me an advice for which I have ever since had occasion to bless God. 'If you desire to be extensively useful, do not spend your time and strength in contending for or against such things as are of a disputable nature, but in testifying against open and notorious vice and in prompting real spiritual holiness.' Let us keep to this, leaving a thousand disputable points to those that have no better business than to toss the ball of controversy to and fro, and let us bear a faithful testimony in our several stations against all ungodliness and unrighteousness, and with all our might recommend that inward and outward holiness without which no man shall see the Lord."

It may be, as I have said, that in talent, in imagination, in learning, in the pure and undefinable quality of genius, Wesley was not the equal of many of his contemporaries; but which among them all equalled him in versatility of beneficence, in zeal of self-sacrifice, in the munificence of his generosity, or in the lustre of the example which he has left to all the world? Consider his supreme disinterestedness, his unparalleled courage, his indefatigable toils. How many have there been in all the centuries who made such an absolute offering of his money to God, and, living on less than many a curate's salary, gave away £40,000? Consider, again, his unparalleled courage. How many have shown equal undauntedness? Men admire the courage of the soldier who heads the forlorn hope through the cross-fire of the batteries, of the sailor or of the fireman who, at personal risk, plucks from destruction an imperilled life; but such physical courage is a million times cheaper and more common than that of the scholar, the gentleman, the clergyman, who, in that age, day after day, month after month, year after year, in England, in America, in Scotland, in Wales, in Ireland, even in the Isle of Man, could, voluntarily and out of the pure love of souls, face raging mobs and descend to what was then regarded as the vulgar humiliation of preaching in the open air. And higher even than this was the moral and spiritual courage which, in the calm of blameless innocence, could treat the most atrocious and the most persistent calumnies with the disdainful indifference of unblemished rectitude. When even Charles Wesley was thrown into a fever of agonized excitement by the scandal against his brother caused by his wife's publication of stolen, forged, or interpolated letters, and wanted him to stay in London and expose the slander, John Wesley remained perfectly calm, knowing that no real harm can befall

> The virtuous mind that ever walks attended
> By a strong-siding champion, Conscience.

"Brother," he said, "when I devoted to God my ease, my time, my life, did I exempt my reputation?" Then consider his indefatigable toils — those sixty-eight years of service; the 4400 miles which he travelled yearly on the execrable roads of those days; the 225,000 miles which he traversed in his lifetime; the 42,400 sermons — sometimes as many as fifteen a week — which he preached even after his return from Georgia — preached mostly in the open air, and sometimes to as many as 20,000 souls; those endless meetings, those burdensome anxieties, those numerous publications, that love of so many communities, continued amid incessant attacks of the mob, the pulpit, and the press, and scarcely ever relaxed till the patriarchal age of eighty-eight. Could a clergyman of any denomination, amid the work which, in comparison to his toils, is but ease and supineness, think it anything but an honour to profess reverence for the memory of one who so heroically lived and so nobly died? Although the world and the Church have learned to be comparatively generous to Wesley now that a hundred years have sped away, and though the roar of contemporary scandal has long since ceased, I doubt whether even now he is at all adequately appreciated. I doubt whether many are aware of the extent to which to this day the impulse to every great work of philanthropy and social reformation has been due to his energy and insight. The British and Foreign Bible Society, the Religious Tract Society, the London Missionary Society, even the Church Missionary Society, owe not a little to his initiative. The vast spread of religious instruction by weekly periodicals, and the cheap press with all its stupendous consequences, were inaugurated by him. He gave a great extension to Sunday-schools and the work of Robert Raikes. He gave a great impulse both to national education and to technical education, and in starting the work of Silas Told, the Foundry Teacher, he anticipated the humble and holy work of John Pounds, the Portsmouth cobbler. He started in his own person the funeral reform, which is only now beginning to attract public attention, when in his will he directed that at his obsequies there should be no hearse, no escutcheon, no coach, no pomp. He visited prisons and ameliorated the lot of prisoners before John Howard; and his very last letter was written to stimulate William Wilberforce in his Parliamentary labours for the emancipation of the slave. When we add to this the revival of fervent worship and devout hymnology among Christian congregations, and their deliverance from the drawling doggerel of Sternhold and Hopkins, and the frigid nullities of Tate and Brady, we have indeed shown how splendid was the list of his achievements, and that, as Isaac Taylor says, he furnished "the starting-point for our modern religious history in all that is characteristic of the present time."

And yet, even in this long and splendid catalogue, we have not mentioned his greatest and most distinctive work, which was that through him to the poor the Gospel was preached. Let Whitefield have the credit of having been the first to make the green grass his pulpit and the heaven his sounding-board; but Wesley instantly followed, at all costs, the then daring example, and, through all evil report and all furious opposition, he continued it until at last, at Kingswood, at the age of eighty-one, he preached in the open air, under the shade of trees which he himself had planted, and surrounded by the children and children's children of his old disciples, who had long since passed away. Overwhelming evidence exists to show what preaching was before and in his day; overwhelming evidence exists to show what the Church and people of England were before and in his day — how dull, how vapid, how soulless, how Christless was the preaching; how torpid, how Laodicean was the Church, how godless, how steeped in immorality was the land. To Wesley was mainly granted the task, for which he was set apart by the hands of invisible consecration, the task which even an archangel might have envied him, of awakening a mighty revival of religious life in those dead pulpits, in that slumbering Church, in that corrupt society. His was the religious sincerity which not only founded the Wesleyan community, but, working through the heart of the very Church which had despised him, flashed fire into her whitening embers. Changing its outward forms, the work of John Wesley caused first the Evangelical movement, then the High Church movement; and, in its enthusiasm of humanity, has even reappeared in all that is best in the humble Salvationists, who learned from the example of Wesley what Bishop Lightfoot called "that lost secret of Christianity, the compulsion of human souls." Recognizing no utterance of authority as equally supreme with that which came to him from the Sinai of conscience, Wesley did the thing and scorned the consequence. His was the voice which offered hope to the despairing and welcome to the outcast. His was the voice which, sounding forth over the Valley of Dry Bones, cried, "Come from the four winds, O breath, and breathe upon these slain that they may live." The poet says:

> Of those three hundred grant but three
> To make a new Thermopylæ.

And when I think of John Wesley, the organizer, of Charles Wesley, the poet, of George

Whitefield, the orator of this mighty movement, I feel inclined to say of those three self-sacrificing and holy men, Grant but even one to help in the mighty work which yet remains to be accomplished! Had we but three such now,

Hoary-headed selfishness would feel
His death-blow, and would totter to his grave;
A brighter light attend the human day,
When every transfer of earth's natural gift
Should be a commerce of good words and works.

We have, it is true, hundreds of faithful workers in the Church of England and in other religious communities. But for the slaying of dragons, the rekindlement of irresistible enthusiasm, the redress of intolerable wrongs, a Church needs many Pentecosts and many Resurrections. And these, in the providence of God, are brought about, not by committees and conferences and common workers, but by men who escape the average; by men who come forth from the multitude; by men who, not content to trudge on in the beaten paths of commonplace and the cart-ruts of routine, go forth, according to their Lord's command, into the highways and hedges; by men in whom the love of God burns like a consuming flame upon the altar of the heart; by men who have become electric to make myriads of other souls thrill with their own holy zeal. Such men are necessarily rare, but God's richest boon to any nation, to any society, to any church, is the presence and work of such a man — and such a man was John Wesley.

The bust placed in Westminster Abbey to the memory of John Wesley, more than twenty years ago, was a very tardy recognition of the vast debt of gratitude which England owes to him. It stands hard by the cenotaph of that other illustrious Nonconformist, Isaac Watts, and gives the beautiful presentment of the aged face of the evangelist and the fine features of Charles, his poet-brother. In the solemn aisle thousands of visitors to our great Temple of Silence and Reconciliation may read three of his great sayings — one, so full of holy energy, "I look on all the world as my parish"; another, so full of bright and holy confidence, "God buries his workmen, but continues his work"; the third, when, on his death-bed, uplifting victoriously his feeble and emaciated arm, he said: "The best of all is, God is with us." "Yes!" he exclaimed again, in a tone of victorious rapture, "the best of all is, God is with us."

IX

JONATHAN EDWARDS

IX

JONATHAN EDWARDS

BY THE REV. A. M. FAIRBAIRN, D.D.

JONATHAN EDWARDS is a thinker difficult to appreciate and very easy to misunderstand. His faults lie on the surface, while his merits are to be discovered only by sympathetic study. He is not only the greatest of all the thinkers that America has produced, but also the highest speculative genius of the eighteenth century. What in him was occasional most impressed his own generation and most easily arrests the eye of ours. What in him was permanent retreats from the hands that hastily glean in the field of literature and religion. What most impresses a cocksure and sceptical critic like Mr. Leslie Stephen is the awfulness of Edwards's descriptions of sin and its punishment; and he marvels that any writer could say anything concerning him without dwelling on his doctrine of hell. But the grim and terrible sermons which Stephen quotes as if they were the essence of Edwards's mind were not the creations of his reason, which was Edwards's master faculty, but the work of his imagination in a peculiar mood — as it were epic pictures thrown out while it was intoxicated with a spiritual passion or drenched by the wave of religious enthusiasm then rolling over New England. In truth, the distinctive theology of Edwards was of quite another order, the creation of a reason all alive with speculative passion, and moved as if by an infinite hunger for the divine. In him religious affection was exalted and transfigured by an illuminative yet inexorable reason, a thought that, urged by the necessity of its own being, could know no rest till it had, not simply grasped the skirts, but, as it were, penetrated to the very heart of deity. In a far higher degree than Spinoza he was a "God-intoxicated man," and his religious affection more than Spinoza's intellectual love made man one in will through being one in heart with God. The development from Edwards emphasized too much what was occasional, while it emphasized too little what was permanent; and so the New England becomes more a scholastic than a speculative theology, while, if it had been true to the genius and soul of Edwards, it would have been more speculative and less scholastic.

In the attempt to understand him we have first to realize the comparative isolation in which he lived, and therefore the independence with which he worked. If we put him back into his time without recollection of his place, no man could seem less the son of his century. He was born in 1703, a year before Locke died. In England deism had commenced its belligerent and barren career. Berkeley had entered Trinity College, and was jotting down in his commonplace book the speculations that were later to become a new "Theory of Vision," and furnish the "Principles of Human Knowledge." Toland was busy proving Christianity not mysterious, and arguing for a new theism which should make God all in all. Of those who may be regarded as more strictly his contemporaries, Joseph Butler entered Oriel College, Oxford, just about the time Edwards entered Yale. David Hume, eight years his junior, became, like Edwards, a student of Locke, but, unlike him, so interpreted Locke as to deduce from him a system of universal doubt, which did not, like that of Descartes, spare thought and find through the ego a way into reasoned belief. In France, in the very year of Edwards's birth, Voltaire entered, a boy of nine, the great Jesuit School, the Collège Louis le Grand, and began to prepare himself to conduct his crusade — in its essence more Christian than those of the Middle Ages — against the tyranny of the unreal and make-believe in religion. While Edwards was pastor in Northampton Rousseau was indulging himself in all the luxury of sentiment, and feeling his way towards the limitation of the individual and the construction of society through the "Social Contract." As Edwards, diffident in secular things while greatly daring in intellectual, was describing to the corporation of Princeton his "peculiarly unhappy constitution, attended with flaccid solids, vapid, siezy, and scarce fluids, and a low tide of spirits; often occasioning a kind of childish weakness and contemptibleness of speech, presence, and demeanour, with a disagreeable dulness and stiffness, much unfitting me for conversation, but more especially for the government of a college," and hesitating to accept the position offered to him — a younger contemporary in Germany, Lessing, was turning his thoughts to the reform of the theatre, and to a more scientific interpretation of religion and its history.

But Edwards in his New England home lived apart from all these European movements and influences. They could, indeed, hardly be said to have touched him. As a student he had studied the " Essay on the Human Understanding," and through it discovered at once his faculty and problem. In Dr. Samuel Johnson of Stratford, and in Cutler, his tutor, he had met men who knew something of Berkeley; the former, in particular, being a convinced idealist. And, indeed, while he was beginning his career as a pastor, Berkeley was attempting to make a home for himself in Rhode Island. But while there are points where he coincides with Berkeley, Edwards's development was independent; they agree rather by logical coincidence than by literary or speculative imitation. And this is the more significant as the agreements are mainly on points which Berkeley later developed, and where he agreed with Malebranche. Edwards, indeed, largely worked out his problems, not only in independence, but in an intellectual isolation which no man in the

Old World could know; least of all was it known to the men with whom he has most affinity — Spinoza, Malebranche, and Berkeley. The shape which both the problems and their solution assumed at his subtle hands proceeded as much from his simple and pure nature as from the simplicity of the life he lived. The faith of his people possessed him. Time was to him eternal; every year, every day, and every hour were the dwelling-place of God. The God he believed in moved all things, filled all time and every place. Yet his individual existence was not a mere moment in the being of the Eternal, but a means by which God realized his purposes in time and fulfilled his ends for eternity. We have to remember, then, at the outset, these two things: (1) the simplicity and purity, yet intense rationality, of Edwards's nature; and (2) the traditional faith, which made all nature supernatural, that possessed and inspired him. From this point of view the things that are most significant of Edwards are not his deliberate and elaborate, but his most spontaneous, thoughts — those that came to him, as it were, by the way of intuition or meditation rather than by the method of logic and evidence. As indicating the quality of his nature, which is in a measure the hidden law of his mind, we may cite two things :

(1) Some of the resolutions he wrote before his nineteenth year :

" Resolved, Never to do any manner of thing, whether in soul or body, less or more, but what tends to the glory of God, nor be nor suffer it, if I can possibly avoid it.

" Resolved, to live with all my might, while I do live.

" Resolved, Never to do anything which I should be afraid to do if it were the last hour of my life.

" Resolved, Never to count that a prayer nor to let that pass as a prayer, nor that as a petition of a prayer, which is so made that I cannot hope that God will answer it."

The fine love of reality in the last resolution is specially noteworthy.

(2) This extract from his diary will show his innate mysticism, the degree in which he was possessed of the passion for the divine :
" Once, as I rode out into the woods for my health, in 1737, having alighted from my horse in a retired place, as my manner commonly has been, to walk for divine contemplation and

prayer, I had a view, that for me was extraordinary, of the glory of the Son of God, as Mediator between God and man, and his wonderful, great, full, pure, and sweet grace and love, and meek and gentle condescension. This grace that appeared so calm and sweet appeared also great above the heavens. The Person of Christ appeared ineffably excellent, with an excellency great enough to swallow up all thought and conception — which continued, as near as I can judge, about an hour; which kept me the greater part of the time in a flood of tears, and weeping aloud. I felt an ardency of soul to be, what I know not otherwise how to express, emptied and annihilated; to lie in the dust, and to be full of Christ alone; to love him with a holy and pure love; to trust in him; to live upon him; to serve and follow him; and to be perfectly sanctified and made pure, with a divine and heavenly purity. I have several other times had views very much of the same nature, and which have had the same effects."

Let us now see how a man with so intense and spiritual a nature as Edwards', and yet so speculative and rational a mind, possessed also of a faith so intense and elevated, and so completely isolated from the great intellectual currents of the time — wrestled in thought with its largest problems. We begin with some of the positions that he lays down while quite a young student as the result of his study of Locke. Locke's analysis of the process of knowledge led him to this — that the ultimate source of ideas was sensation; that sensation was due to the operation of external bodies, and the quality which remained to the external body in the ultimate analysis was Resistance, which is only another form of Descartes's Extension. But Edwards translates Locke's resistance into a mode of divine energy or will, thus : " There is nothing out of the mind but Resistance, and as Resistance is nothing else than the actual exertion of God's power, so the power can be nothing else than the constant Law or Method of that actual exertion." Matter and energy are thus transformed into the being and will of God ; and so he again says : " Nor will it be found that the principles we lay down at all make void natural philosophy, or the science of the Causes or Reasons of corporeal changes ; for to find out the reasons of things, in natural philosophy, is only to find out the proportion of God's acting." He further thinks that all the natural changes in the universe which follow in a continued series "do not perhaps exist anywhere perfectly but in the Divine Mind." "But, then, if it be inquired, what exists in the Divine Mind; and how these things exist there? I answer, There is his determination, his care, and his design, that ideas shall be united for ever, just so, and in such a manner, as is agreeable to such a series. For instance, all the ideas that ever were, or ever shall be to all eternity, in any created mind, are answerable to the existence of such a peculiar Atom in the beginning of the Creation, of such a determinate figure and size, and to have such a motion given to it: That is, they are all such as Infinite Wisdom sees would follow according to the series of nature, from such an Atom, so moved."

We feel as if we were reading the first and second books of Spinoza's "Ethics" through the psychology of Locke as modified by Berkeley. Edwards we may here term a monotheistic idealist, with the emphasis on the *mono*. The order of things we term nature is the order of ideas in the mind of God, and this becomes our order of ideas by the direct operation of the creative mind. And so it follows that mind is primary; indeed, in a sense there is nothing but mind and its ideas, those of man being effects from those of God. In words that suggest Kant he says: "*Place itself* is mental, and *Within* and *Without* are mere mental conceptions. . . . When I say the Material Universe exists only in the mind, I mean that it is absolutely dependent on the conception of the mind for its existence, and does not exist as Spirits do, whose existence does not consist in, nor in dependence on, the conception of other minds. . . . Things, as to God, exist from all Eternity, alike ; that is, the idea is always the same, and after the same mode. The existence of things, therefore, that are not actually in created minds, consist only in Power, or in the Determination of God, that such and such ideas shall be raised in creative minds, upon such conditions." He sums up his philosophical position in these remarkable words (the italics are his own) : " That which truly is the Substance of all Bodies, is *the infinitely exact, and precise, and perfectly stable Idea, in God's mind, together with his stable Will, that the same shall gradually be communicated to us, and to other minds, according to certain fixed and exact established Methods and Laws;* or, in somewhat different language, *the infinitely exact and precise Divine*

Idea, together with an answerable, perfectly exact, precise, and stable Will, with respect to correspondent communications to Created Minds, and effects on their minds." [1] Nature thus becomes the continuous creation of God; all our knowlege is the result of his action, and in the interpretation of what is without we are only really discovering the secret of what is within by thinking the thoughts of God after him.

Let us see now how he works this fundamental idea out into a theology. And first as to his conception of Deity, which also involves that of the relation which He sustains to the universe. Edwards, then, formulates the principle that "God and real existence are the same; God is, and there is none else." This is logically involved in his theory both of being and of knowing. For as real existence is ideal, the divine as the fontal or creative mind is the source of all ideas, and is therefore the reality

---

[1] Compare with the quotations in the text the following propositions from Spinoza's "Ethics": "Præter deum nulla dari neque concipi potest substantia," "quicquid est in Deo est, et nihil sine Deo esse neque concipi potest." "Deus non tantum est causa efficiens rerum existentia, sed etiam essentiæ." "Voluntas non potest vocari causa libera, sed tantum necessaria." "Ordo et connexio idearum idem est, ac ordo et connexio rerum."

of all existence. And so he later expresses his notion thus: "The eternal and infinite Being is, in effect, being in general, and comprehends universal existence." And, again, he says: God is "the foundation and fountain of all being and all perfection, from whom all is perfectly derived, and on whom all is most absolutely and perfectly dependent; whose being and beauty is, as it were, the sum and comprehension of all existence and excellence much more than the sun is the fountain and summary comprehension of all the light and brightness of the day." But as God is, such must the creation be, for as is the fountain such is the stream, as is the beginning such is the end. And so he describes the end of the creation as really contained within the divine nature. "It appears reasonable to suppose," he says, "that it was God's last end that there might be a glorious and abundant emanation of his infinite fulness of good *ad extra*, or without himself; and that the disposition to communicate himself, or diffuse his own *Fulness*, was what moved him to create the world." As the end for which the world was created is thus contained in God, and as creation is "an emanation of his own infinite fulness," it follows that as He is, its end must be; and this end he describes in twofold terms — as his own glory or as the creature's good, but these as coincident and identical, not as different, still less as opposed. Thus he says : " God's respect to the creature's good and his respect to himself is not a divided respect; but both are united in one, as the happiness of the creature aimed at is happiness in union with himself." And again: " Thus it is easy to conceive how God should seek the good of the creature, consisting in the creature's knowledge of holiness, and even his happiness, from a supreme regard to *himself;* as his happiness arises from that which is an image and participation of God's own beauty; and consists in the creature's exercising a supreme regard to God, and complacence in him."

So far we have been concerned with his conception of God, and God's relation to the course and end of being; we have now to see how he translated his theology into religion. Religion was to him essentially imitation of God, the godly being the godlike man. As, then, God was, such ought the virtuous man to be. The methods and ends of the good were those of God. As to God, "he delights in his own goodness, and in the exercise of his goodness, and therefore he delights to make the creature happy, and delights to see him made happy." He says: "In God, the love of himself and the love of the public are not to be distinguished as in man, because God's being, as it were, comprehends all." He means, then, that as man's obedience expresses God's perfection, the divine glory is manifested in the character and the conduct of the saints; for "they are all but the emanations of God's glory, or the excellent brightness and fulness of the Divinity diffused, overflowing, and, as it were, enlarged; or, in one word, existing *ad extra*." Since religion is imitation of such a Deity, he conceives virtue " as love to the greatest happiness, or love to the happiness of universal being"; *i.e.*, the virtuous man is the man whose conduct is governed by the very end for which God made the world. For it is not merely personal happiness or love to our own personal pleasure which constitutes an action virtuous; on the contrary, he thus admirably distinguishes: "That which is often called *Self-love* is exceedingly improperly called *Love*, for they do not only say that one loves himself, when he sees something amiable in himself, the view of which begets delight. But merely an inclina-

M

tion to pleasure, and averseness to pain, they call Self-love; so that the devils and other damned spirits love themselves, not because they see anything in themselves which they imagine to be lovely, but merely because they do not incline to pain, but to pleasure." True virtue, therefore, "consists in love for God, the being of beings infinitely the greatest and best." It is not the love of pleasure but the happiness that is holiness — a certain kind of beautiful nature which appears in itself beautiful or comely because it so makes comeliness — is godlike because it tends to make the world like God.

While these are Edwards's fundamental and characteristic ideas, the heart as it were of his philosophy, they are modified in the working out by the formal logic and the imperfect psychology which he owed to Locke. When he turned from speculation to experience, he looked at it through the traditional beliefs of his people. These were, of course, imbedded in the very speech of his community, the local conditions from which he could not extricate himself, as it were the vernacular into which he had been born. From this point of view we may regard the "Treatise on the Will" as not so much a creation of his philosophy as a theological inheritance; but its justification was altogether in his own manner. It is remarkable that while in his ultimate thinking he had so completely emancipated himself from empiricism, in this field of thought he identified himself with the school to which he was most radically opposed. For just as Collins had so developed Locke as to deny liberty and affirm necessity, and as Hume had resolved causation into mere antecedence and sequence, and as Henry Home had applied the same principles to the naturalistic explanation of morality and religion, so Edwards, in his " Treatise on the Will," turned his back upon his own philosophy and advocated one alien not only to Christianity but even to theism. This may require a word of explanation. His fundamental notion that God is the only real cause may be made the basis of a theory of necessity, but then the necessity that it expresses will be one of universal benevolence. It may be quite victoriously argued that where God is the essence and energy of all that is, man cannot be free; but if God be conceived as so good as to will universal happiness, the ultimate end must be even as his will. It is remarkable that the thinker who had, on the most transcendental of all subjects, so broken with empiricism, should, at this point of transcendent practical importance, have fallen such a potent and willing victim to its exhausted charms. But we can see how it happened. The psychological basis of the Treatise Locke supplied. The will was identified with desire, choice with inclination. As desire always must be for the agreeable and towards the pleasant, so the will is always as the strongest motive is. Choice, in other words, was superseded by inclination, and where inclination or desire is the only form of choice the man is but the victim of circumstances, made according to what happens to him rather than according to what he is. The "Treatise on the Will" was Edwards's most elaborate work; it was also his most immediately influential. It was received in Scotland, to the dismay of his evangelical friends, with warm approval by their freethinking contemporaries. Henry Home and David Hume found their own ideas here expanded and enforced by the champion of the orthodox, and the latter, in dismay, turned to him for explanations of difficulties, which indeed he attempted to give even while he failed to perceive their real source and significance. We may leave the Treatise to its empirical admirers, while holding to the theology which is its corrective and negation.

Edwards was in many ways a man who exemplified the most characteristic qualities of New England. Occasionally, through his all too sombre speech, a kindly gleam of humour breaks. Thus he quaintly says, "Although the devil be exceedingly crafty and subtle, yet he is one of the greatest fools and blockheads in the world, as the subtlest of wicked men are. Sin is of such a nature that it strangely infatuates and stultifies the mind." Take him all in all, in the beauty of his character, in the elevation of his thought, his claim to stand amid the great thinkers of the world is indisputable. In England here we have just been making welcome the new edition of Bishop Butler's works — edited by the statesman who in his retirement shows his undiminished vigour and reveals his lifelong interest in theology — and I have been comparing Butler's answer to Tindal with Edwards's, with the result that I am forced to confess that while the rigour and vigour of inexorable logic and the strength which comes from a concentration due to the careful exclusion of all irrelevant matter are with Butler, the elevation, the insight, the oversight, the feeling of the magnitude of the problem, and the forecast of the lines along which the ultimate answer must move are all with Edwards. Still, he speaks to us in a strange tongue. It is, indeed, our mother speech, yet, as it were, in a dialect so remote from the culture of Europe, from the elegance of literature, and the discipline of the classics, that we hardly know it as our own; but when we have penetrated under the speech to the matter, and behind the form to the man, we are fain to confess that in this lone New Englander, preaching now in Northampton, whether amid the excitement of the Great Revival or in the face of the coldness of an estranged people, and now labouring in the backwoods at Stockbridge, amid Indians and amid countrymen ruder than the Indians, we yet have one who holds his place amid the most honourable of the doctors of the Church, of the philosophers of his century, and of the saints of God.

X

HORACE BUSHNELL

X

HORACE BUSHNELL

BY THE REV. T. T. MUNGER, D.D.

HORACE BUSHNELL appeared at a time when a theologian was greatly needed in New England. The force of Edwards's influence had spent itself, or, rather, its soul had gone to feed an intellectual idealism, and its body had degenerated into a hard formalism. His overwhelming sense and assertion of God — a thing not easily brought within the limits of theology or philosophy as they are usually regarded — had lost its inspiring power.

When Dr. Bushnell began his ministry in Hartford in 1833, the churches may be said to have been living under a system rather than under truths. I will not use my limited space to enforce the distinction, though it is one of real importance. The good qualities that we ascribe to the churches of that day grew out of the truths involved in their theological system; their faults sprang out of their insistence that those truths must be so defined and shaped as to form a coherent system. It was a marvel of exactness — definitions and proof-texts being accepted — but it never satisfied the thinkers, and was constantly being "improved." In its last form it reposes in unpublished manuscripts or unread volumes. But, though undergoing constant modification, it was imposed on the churches with relentless rigour as the substance of their faith. Its conceptions of God and man were alike defective, its exegesis was poor and arbitrary, its logic formal and pedantic, and its conclusions were often inhuman. While involving great nourishing truths, it so combined them that they almost ceased to wear the Christian cast. It is too well known to require statement — a fall in Adam, who in some sense contained or represented the race; a consequent universal condemnation to eternal punishment; an atonement that either endured the punishment or made some corresponding expression of it; imputed sin and imputed righteousness; electing grace and reprobation, each irrespective of character except as it may have been anticipated in the counsels of eternity. Such, in substance, was the theology that prevailed in the early part of the century. As we now see things, it interpreted hardly a fact pertaining to God or man or Scripture or nature with correctness, and yet it asserted dogmas that presumed an exhaustive knowledge of them. Great Biblical words like *faith* and *sacrifice* and *life* were emptied of their real meaning and made to carry a sense not intended. Texts were taken out of their setting and used in support of doctrines to which they do not refer; and thus the whole Bible was subordinated to a system which only by a fiction could be said to have its origin in it. It was mainly designed to set forth the sovereignty and the glory of God — in redemption indeed, but the two terms were put in such a relation that redemption was belittled by sovereignty and actually failed in reflecting glory — a mistake in the construction of the system that has reacted fatally upon it. The mistake was a natural one; the idea of humanity and of the scope of redemption had not yet fully come.

Our reverence for the fathers leads us to speak of the vanishing away of this system as a change in habit of thought, but it is more than that; it is disappearing because it is no longer regarded as true.

Important but not fundamental changes in it were going on while Bushnell was a student in Yale College. The New Haven divines were urging a view of the freedom of the will and of the moral government of God which developed a deeper sense of human responsibility and induced a revival of Christian activity the effects of which were felt in the birth of great religious enterprises that are still full of power — an indication of emergence from the prevailing theology. But it was a period of fierce controversy. Dr. Taylor and Dr. Tyler were dividing the churches over a metaphysical notion of the will, the difference between them being that one claimed that it was a little freer than the other; and the degree of difference was thought to involve results derogatory to God and harmful to souls The condition, intellectually and morally, was cluttered with metaphysical distinctions, emanating from the studies of men imperfectly educated, but keen enough to see the lack of adjustment in a system which showed such lack because it was made up of truths which could not be dovetailed into each other. The pulpit was narrow and timid for fear of getting beyond the imposed conditions, or it was tyrannical in its insistence on them. The distinctions and differences had been growing since Edwards, and had reached a stage which Bushnell described in his preface to "Christ in Theology" as "the sedimentary subsidence of theology itself, precipitated in the confused mixture of its elements." Meanwhile in Massachusetts the Unitarian schism had paralyzed Orthodoxy with fear, and no one dared to speak above one's breath. Professor Park had not yet come to Andover with his great word — one of the most effective ever spoken in the American pulpit — on "The Theology of the Intellect and the Feelings" — effective because it showed a way out of an over-rigid theology; a kind Providence provides such vents for intolerable beliefs.

What made this condition so deplorable, and so exasperating to Dr. Bushnell when he became a pastor, was that this system was carried into and imposed on religious experience. The Thirty-nine Articles are Calvinistic, but they are not intruded on the life of the Episcopal laity: wise but illogical. The clergy of New England could not endure such inconsistency. Indeed, they had nothing to fall back on if their dogmas were set aside; they had no function but to turn them into experience; the cardinal duty of the pulpit was to preach them. And well was it carried out — an honest but doubtful business. Religious experience was made to tally with the system and run the round of its several members in a fixed order. Human life in all its complexity and variety was forced to act under a sharply defined conception of lost condition by nature, heavy conviction of sin, struggle, surrender, illumination by the Spirit, to be followed by an experience of constant heart-searching with possible doubts of election and never any certainty of it, fear lest the sin against the Holy Ghost had been committed, alternations of peace and assurance with occasional ecstasies of trust and hope; but as a whole the experience was overshadowed by morbid misgiving and painful foreboding — a Puritan search for the Holy Grail.

The experience was adjusted to a system every feature of which must be reproduced by every person; but while all were thus held to the system with but small room for the play of personal qualities, the experience was absolutely individual: each soul was isolated from every other, and almost from God, and left to wrestle alone for salvation. This emphasis upon system lay at the root of the New England zeal for orthodoxy, and of its intolerance of the slightest departure from it. If one doubted any part, one doubted the whole. If he doubted the eternity of punishment, he endangered the moral government of God ; if he doubted decrees, all theology was involved in confusion : both doubts were an impeachment of the sovereignty of God.

Such was the condition of things when Dr. Bushnell came upon the stage. Its main feature was its unnaturalness. Each member of the system represented or hinted at a truth, but the truths were so defined and manipulated that their real meaning evaporated and left only a travesty of the Gospel. The system bore little relation to human nature, took no account of its variety or need, or method of action, but loaded it with burdens which did not belong to it, and then required it to throw them off by processes that were arbitrary and unnatural.

Dr. Bushnell was reared and educated under this system, though some exceptional influences in childhood separated him somewhat from its more rigid features. He never broke away from it externally, but from the first he protested against it. He refused to think under it or along its lines, and the point of his stoutest protest was its unnaturalness. He took the path by which superior minds have always found their way into new realms of truth. They do not pass from one school to another, but instead rise into some new or some larger conception of nature and start afresh. All gains in philosophy and religion and civilization have been made by farther inroads into nature, and never in any other way. Dr. Bushnell, with the unerring instinct of a discoverer, struck this path and kept it to the end. At the bottom of all his work lies a profound sense of nature, of its meaning and force in the realm of the spirit. He did not deny a certain antithesis between nature and the supernatural, but he so defined the latter that the two could be embraced in the one category of nature when viewed as the ascertained order of God in creation. The supernatural is simply the realm of freedom, and it is as natural as the physical realm of necessity. Thus he not only got rid of the traditional antinomy between them, but led the way into that conception of the relation of God to his world which more and more is taking possession of modern thought. In his essay on Language he says (and the thought is always with him as a governing principle): "The whole universe of nature is a perfect analogon of the whole universe of thought or spirit. Therefore, as nature becomes truly a universe only through science revealing its universal laws, the true universe of thought and spirit cannot sooner be conceived." Thus he actually makes the revelation of spiritual truth wait on the unfolding of the facts and laws of the world of nature. There is something pathetic in the attitude of this great thinker sitting in the dark, waiting for disclosures in nature that would substantiate what he felt was true in the realm of the spirit. A generation later he would have seen the light for which he longed — a light that justifies the central point of all his main contentions.

He seems to have taken to heart the fact that God made the heavens and earth and all that in them is. This sense of nature was largely an endowment. No theologian was ever more fully dowered with the seeing eye and the interpreting mind. He was a poet before he was a theologian, and his chief excellence as the latter is due to his greatness as the former. This divine gift was stimulated and directed by Coleridge, whose "Aids to Reflection" kindled within him a passion for thought and feeling early in his career. Thus, without being fully aware of it, he was in close accord with that modern habit of theological thought which came in through Coleridge and has since pervaded the theological world. Its key is nature; its secret is reason. It sees first and speculates afterward. Dr. Bushnell's entire work may be characterized as a plea for naturalness. His eye is always fixed on the nature of things. His first book — "Christian Nurture" — is a plea for Christian education according to nature, as seen in the divine constitution of the family. "God in Christ" and "Christ in Theology" are attempts to bring the Trinity within conceptions that do not violate nature. His Sabellianism grew out of his desire to bring the Trinity under the great principle of the Logos, and so get God out of his incomprehensibility down into a region where things are a revelation of God; the Logos is the meeting-ground of God and nature, the visible side of the invisible God. In Christ God manifests himself as human, and feels and acts and suffers in human ways, but it is all divine and yet natural as these processes in man are natural.

"Nature and the Supernatural" had for its purpose to include the two contrasted domains within one category. The will itself, he claimed, was a supernatural agent. "The Vicarious Sacrifice" was an effort to state the Atonement in terms that are justified in human experience. His essays are careful explorations into the nature and relations of the thing under discussion; often they ran wild with imagination, but in the farthest flights he never let go of the guiding clue of nature.

The times had much to do with the development and shaping of his powers. He began his ministry just as that crisis was maturing which ended the reign of superstition and tradition, and ushered in the scientific habit of thought. It was a time well described in Matthew Arnold's lines:

> Wandering between two worlds;
> One dead, the other powerless to be born.

Bushnell felt the deadness of one world, but not the inability of the other to be born.

Born he at least would be, and his whole life was one steady effort to find his way into this new world where highest truths could be joined to highest reason by the connecting bond of nature. Nearly everything that he wrote was grounded "in principles interpreted by human analogies." The power and greatness of the man lay in the fact that he was broad enough to cover the world in which he first found himself, and also that into which he made his way. He did not abjure his past; he made no violent break with the existing order; the weakness of schism was not in him; he might be turned out, but he would not himself go out. His historic sense was strong, as it is with all great men, and he shrank from violating it by external change. The past contained great realities of faith and practice, and he held fast to them. He had no liking for raw and violent denials and fresh-made doctrines. But while he held to the past, he played the part of critic with vigour, cleared it of its hardness and narrowness and superstition, searched out "the soul of goodness" in it, and so paved the way into a world as new as that of which Arnold sadly dreamed.

I do not mean that Dr. Bushnell wholly parted

with what now seem to us imperfect and provincial opinions in theology, nor that his thought was always what would now be regarded as scientific; no man ever wholly frees himself from the defects of his age; but he found his way into the world of the spirit. Instead of leaving one field and going over into another, he rose into a higher region that spanned both. The characteristic of the man was spirituality; his ruling passion was for freedom and order. He found his way into freedom along two paths — one by which he "passed into the vein of comprehensiveness, questioning whether all parties were not in reality standing for some one side or article of the truth"; the other was a theory of language which he regarded as his own peculiar work. Whether it was a true theory or not, it served his purpose; if it was a hobby, it carried him whither he was moved to go. His biographer regards it as "the key to Horace Bushnell," and, undoubtedly, he is to be read under his own theory of language. Its root is to be found in the ancient doctrine of the Logos. As used by himself, words became the reflection of his thought rather than "exact representatives" of it. This theory seemed necessary to enable him to speak according to his thought on such themes as the Trinity, atonement, miracle, and regeneration — subjects that chiefly engaged his attention. He found these great doctrines tied up and smothered under hard and narrow definitions. His first step was rejection of the definitions; thus he escaped into the world of the spirit, where language does not define but only indicates or shadows forth. The chief value of this theory of language lies in its assertion that spiritual facts and processes cannot be brought within strict definition. We are getting to know this well enough without a special theory. Possibly, however, the day is not yet past when categorical answers to sharply defined questions concerning infinite and eternal things are required of suspected teachers. In such a case a theory of language that eludes the dictum of "the evident meaning of the words" is not only convenient but justifiable, and is a proper defence when official bigotry worries such teachers. Even theology has its humorous side, and Samson may jest while the Philistines torture him. Dr. A——, his chief accuser, spends two days with Dr. Bushnell and is led to believe that there is no heresy in him; he could not understand his host's use of language.

I can but hint at the works which came from his prolific pen — a dozen volumes at least, five of them solid treatises on theology and the rest sermons or essays. There is a logical order in the treatises which indicates that one sprang out of or was rendered necessary by another. He began where theology has so often broken down and started afresh — as Dr. Prentice, of Union Seminary, long ago pointed out — with children, in a treatise on "Christian Nurture." It won all Christian motherhood and well-nigh the fathers, but it was discovered to be heretical, and charges to that effect were brought, which never relaxed but never accomplished anything except to forward the doctrine it attacked. The aim of the book was to establish the proposition: "That the child is to grow up a Christian and never know himself as being otherwise"; a very simple statement, but it shook New England theology to its foundations. It attacked the extreme individualism into which theology had fallen, and recalled it to those organic relations between parents and children which are recognized in all the historic Churches, and are steadily gaining significance under modern thought. Christian experience had become too supernatural; Dr. Bushnell brought it within the range of human nature. The effect of the treatise has been to make Christian character not less a product of divine grace, and to reinforce it by the natural relations of the family. Its main idea is as old as the oldest religion; for no men were ever so dull as to conceive or develop a religion on a basis of pure individualism; but Dr. Bushnell treated the subject in a full and thorough way, and prepared it for the modern conceptions and applications of heredity.

The next book in point of influence is "The Vicarious Sacrifice." I refer only to the first volume, and not to the second, which was originally published under the title "Forgiveness and Law," and afterward incorporated with the first as a part of the same treatise. Its main purpose is to show that the object and issue of the atonement is the moral recovery of man. Christ did not die "to even up a score of penalty," but to make the cross a salvation by its power on life and character. The key to his view is found on the title-page: "The Vicarious Sacrifice, grounded in Principles of Universal Obligation." He regards "the sacrifice and cross of Christ his simple duty, and not any superlative, optional kind of good, outside of all the common principles of virtue. It is not goodness over good, and yielding a surplus of merit in that manner for us, but it is only just as good as it ought to be, or the highest law of right required it to be." Here again we detect the note of nature which is heard in all his writings. He will not admit that there is any principle or law in the atonement which is not of "universal obligation." The sacrifice of Christ meant and called for an exactly corresponding sacrifice on the part of all men; it *impressed* them for that end, and so saved them. It is not penal, nor expiatory except as it works morally to overcome evil, nor is it an expedient to uphold a moral government. These extra-human renderings of a simple and universal moral law are set aside to make room for one that the twentieth century will hardly call in question. No efforts to link this view with those found in the old theologies — doubtless it can be found in them — lessen its novelty as it was propounded to the churches of New

England. As things were in 1866 it was undoubtedly heretical, as many a sympathizing young pastor found to his cost. The volume strengthened the suspicion awakened by "Christian Nurture," and henceforth the heresy connected with him was that of the "moral view." Efforts were made to bring him to trial, but the Congregational system does not readily lend itself to such work, and he suffered only such small penalties as the religious newspapers inflicted, one of which went into a decline under his stinging characterization of it as "not only behind the age, but behind all ages." But he was not much given to controversy or self-defence. Only once or twice did he turn on his accusers, and then it was as with that "two-handed engine that smites once and smites no more." He was too profound a lover of truth to make it matter of debate; he did not so reach his conclusions, nor would he so defend them. He belonged rather to the order of seers, and simply declared what it had been given him to see, and so left it.

Whatever may be said of "The Vicarious Sacrifice" in the way of criticism, the fact remains that it introduced into New England theology the moral view of the atonement, and largely supplanted the existing view. The doctrine now preached in New England, with modifications indeed, and much of independent interpretation, is that which runs through this treatise — a fact recognized in a recent sermon by Professor George Harris, of Andover, in which he said that "his (Dr. Bushnell's) theory is now more generally accepted than any other."

This theory runs through all his books. It was infolded in his first work — "Christian Nurture" — which, indeed, contained the germ of all his writings. This was inevitable. When he struck out the great truth that the Christian training of a child must be in the ways of nature, nature being regarded as God's order, it was inevitable that every doctrine and phase of Christian truth should be treated in like manner. Dr. Bushnell early, and by the very quality of his nature, fell into the scientific habit of thought, and he kept to it throughout. He was often mystical, sometimes inconsistent, but at bottom, in all his conceptions and in almost every sentence, he was scientific; that is, he kept his eye on facts, on the things that are made, on the divine order wrought into the nature of man, and reasoned from them. Therefore, when he came to treat of miracles — an inevitable theme for him — he searched and enlarged the realm of nature to find a place for them. Here again his thought may be at times inaccurate, and without the severity that would now be insisted on, but none the less did he redeem the subject from definitions and interpretations that defied reason and provoked unbelief. He did more; he directed attention to the field where they must be located, and stated the general principles under which they must be regarded; he broke down the artificial barrier between two worlds which are not two but one, and made us see that unity in the works of God which destroys the antithesis between nature and miracle, and brings all into one spiritual category. The purpose of the book is indicated in its title: "Nature and the Supernatural as together Constituting the One System of God." The treatise is still of great value, and is perhaps the best on the subject. The tenth chapter has become a Christian classic. The writer did not have the advantages afforded by recent science. Evolution, which simplifies the treatment of all subjects, was nothing more than a disputed hypothesis; biology was a new science; the new psychology was in its infancy, and exegesis was still enthralled under a hard and narrow doctrine of inspiration. The limitations of the treatise are due to these conditions, but all the more does it reveal the bravery and insight of the author; he anticipated discoveries and wrought the spirit of them into his pages. He hewed out a path through a very tangled wilderness, guided only by his insight into the things of God and by a deep sense of the need of finding a way through. The condition in which the subject lay when Dr. Bushnell began to write was lamentable; it was exactly that reprobated by Christ when the Jews clamoured for a sign. Thus preached, it played fatally into the hands of infidelity, and added to the perplexity of a faith that was already heavily burdened. As on other subjects, he opened a way out, stemming the tide of schismatic denial and rejection by leading men into a region where they could at least think with some show of reason, and look about them with their feet planted on the nature of things. Dr. Bushnell was accounted a heretic, but he saved orthodoxy, at least what of it was worth saving. The churches of New England were fast drifting into a condition where schism or dry-rot would have soon made an end of them. He arrested this process, and rediscovered for them the world of the spirit; he directed their attention to the nature of things, and made them a logos of divine truths; he created a soil for an ethical and reasonable faith, and sowed seed in it that is still yielding ever-increasing harvests.

The recognition of his service was tardy and scant except among the younger clergy. There was, however, a quasi-recognition in the distinction that was made between his sermons and his treatises; the latter were generally set down as dangerous, but the former were acknowledged to be full of spiritual power and comfort. The distinction but showed the pitiful state of criticism at the time; it was kind but weak. The sermons and the treatises grew out of each other, and were but forms of the same thing. But lack of recognition is a trifling matter; the true prophet is aware that it must be so. It was not a specially sore thing to Dr. Bushnell. He was immensely stored with inner resources. He delighted in his own thoughts, and he found his way into that hidden world where he "fed on God" (his own phrase), and so had strength and health of soul. Late in life he said to a friend, "I have been greatly blessed in my doubtings." In New

England, and not less in Great Britain, a more Christlike Gospel is preached, and Christian believers the world over are living in the exercise and comfort of a more rational faith, because of the work he did.

He was a solitary thinker. His writings lack the signs of full contact with the scholastic world; and perhaps they are all the better for it. They suggest by their style and form that he thought as he wrote, and that he worked his way along to his conclusions instead of starting with a full plan. Hence he often found it necessary to qualify and correct what he had said, and so his writings have a prolixity that might have been avoided.

The real greatness of Bushnell does not consist in his strictly theological work, but in those separate and yet connected spiritual revelations in which his life abounded. Read his books — treatise or essay or sermon — and it is not the truth of thought that most impresses you, but the truth of experience. He was preeminently a thinker, but he was still more a practical man in the realm of the spirit. A man of affairs, of keen worldly insight and wisdom, he carried this quality into the things of the spirit. He had no "unrelated facts," as every title-page and every chapter shows. His apprehension of God in his personal experience, the play of his own spirit back and forth in God, his moral interpretation of life and of history, his ready perception of the divinest truths in his daily walks, his easy and natural lifting of the earthly into the heavenly, and bringing the powers of eternity down into the commonest events of life — these things constitute the greatness and power of the man. In his life as well as in his writings he overcame the hard dualism he found in the prevailing theology, and became himself a revelation of the oneness of God in the world of the spirit and in nature.

The limits of this article permit no mention of Dr. Bushnell as a preacher, nor of the varied work which he performed in other fields than theology, nor of the incidents of his life. I cannot spread out in detail his character, in which virility, mental vigour, saintliness, common sense, imagination, and spiritual insight waged no war with one another, but instead conspired to produce a man who stands on the same plane with Edwards and Channing and Emerson — the other great teachers of the life of the spirit whom New England has produced.

XI

FREDERICK DENISON MAURICE

XI

FREDERICK DENISON MAURICE

BY THE REV. A. V. G. ALLEN, D.D.

THERE are some voices which are impersonal, speaking, as it were, out of the darkness, giving no hint of time or place, and gaining nothing in power or directness by a study of their environment. Such was Thomas à Kempis, whose message comes with equal force to every age. Something of this quality was in Maurice, imparting to his thought a certain enduring appeal, as if he belonged to no particular time or country, or had received no special influence from his surroundings. And yet no man ever lived more deeply in the heart of his generation, and his teaching contains a profound response to the immediate needs of the hour.

The world into which he entered seemed to be losing its hold on God. Among his more eminent contemporaries, Carlyle complained that God was doing nothing; Mill regarded the divine existence as an open question, and Darwin appeared to have lost his religious faculty. It was a world interested in reform, whose watchwords were liberalism and progress, whose programme called for the removal of ancient abuses, under which were included religion and the Church. In the place of these relics of a bygone age, science was offered and the religion of humanity, as if adequate substitutes. Agitations were rife for the improvement of social conditions; but the leaders, for the most part, had ceased to look to God for aid or inspiration — it was time at last that men should help themselves. The labouring men, with their grievances, turned away from the Church and the means of grace as if they were empty mockeries. The higher walks of thought and culture were invaded with religious doubt, a mood in which men would fain believe but could not. The negation had gone deeper than in the eighteenth century, when men professed, at least, to believe in natural religion, and when on this ground Bishop Butler had met them with his Analogy. Now natural religion was called in question; it had become the issue whether God existed or the soul of man was immortal. Efforts were not wanting to meet the situation — proposed reconstructions of the Church after antique models which had once been useful, or the presentation of the claims of the Roman Church as somehow strangely adapted to the requirements of the hour.

These were the problems of the age to which Maurice appealed with the conviction that "no man," as he had said of Coleridge, "will ever be of much use to his generation who does not apply himself mainly to the questions which are agitating those who belong to it." It was the burden of his message that God was manifesting himself in the contemporary world of human thought and activity. "The knowledge of God," he wrote, "I regarded as the key to all other knowledge, as that which connected knowledge with life." And again, "The only way to consider philosophy is in connection with the life of the world, and not as a set of merely intellectual speculations and systems." The light of the world was first revealed in life, and life was the light of men.

The preparation of Maurice for his mission as a theologian began in his early years, as a child in the household. His father was a Unitarian minister, with a simple, genial creed whose principal tenet was the fatherhood of God; his mother was a Calvinist, thinking of God as absolute sovereign will without whose decree of election salvation was impossible, and for herself doubting if her name were enrolled among the elect. Maurice was forced by his filial love and respect, no less than by his sympathetic nature, but also by his spiritual insight, to live in the creed of both his parents, and was thus early called to mediate between religious attitudes that seemed to neutralize each other.

His method of solving the difficulty was a simple one. He insisted that both creeds should be understood as expressing realities or existing relationships, not merely analogies of human reasoning or notions of the mind which it was pleased to entertain. When thus interpreted, the reconciliation followed — the absolute Sovereign of the universe, whose will was inflexible, was at the same time the Infinite Father whose love was the inmost essence of his being. If no one could escape from the control of absolute and sovereign Will, so also no one could be excluded from the love of the Eternal Father. The range of fatherhood was co-extensive with the energy of the divine will. It expanded before the vision till it included not only the Church but the whole secular world as well. Maurice admitted no distinction between a special and a common grace, for such a distinction was incompatible with the idea of fatherhood. Preterition or reprobation as defined in the language of the schools were not fit expressions for describing the economy of the divine will, which was also a father's love. Everywhere it was the same God, call him the Infinite Father or the sovereign Will, who condemned the evil and inspired the good. The loving providence or the infinite purpose of existence must therefore be revealed in every sphere of human life, in the Church and in religion, but also in philosophy and literature, in art and science, in politics and in the social order.

But, further, the relationship of God to the world, since it was an actual or real relationship and not a notion begotten by the mind, must still exist apart from and despite its latency to the consciousness. The energizing of the divine will was not dependent upon human acknowledgment nor limited in its activity by human recognition. The fatherhood of God, embracing in its scope every child of man, was the latent reality which gave significance to baptism or invested with a deeper meaning the process of conversion. If there were danger that the doctrine of the divine fatherhood might be misinterpreted to sanction laxity or indulgence, yet, when conjoined in organic unity with sovereign will, the love of God became the supreme principle of moral law; righteousness was seen as the inmost essence of the loving purpose which has gone forth into creation ; the fatherhood which demanded righteousness in the children could grant no relaxation, but must seek and surely find its accomplishment through manifold agencies in life, through chastisement or the bitter agony of experience whether in this world or in another. If the moral purpose of God does not always appear in direct manifestation, yet indirectly it never fails to be revealed in the confusion and misery which await the infringement of the moral law. The existence of evil was the one subject upon which Maurice refused to speculate. But while he did not inquire why sin should have entered the world, he dwelt upon the experience that condemned it — how the Bible, the Church, society, and each individual conscience bore witness to its ravages. He recognized also that the normal order of the world and the constitution of man were visibly at war with evil, and since the divine love was revealed in the constitution of things and was also identical with sovereign will, evil must at last be overcome and banished from the universe.

It fell to the lot of Maurice to come into close personal contact with almost every variety of religious thought in England; and, by virtue of that mysterious element in his personality which made him from his childhood a mediator in religious differences, he learned to live, as it were, in the divergent forms of the common household of faith, to feed upon the truth they held, so that he could interpret their mission from within their fold. In this way he accepted the doctrine of the "inner light" as held by the Quakers, while clinging also to the necessity of sacraments and outward form as revealed in the spiritual life of organic historic Christendom. He was thrown among the Irvingites and listened to their urgent cry for the living Spirit who once wrought by signs and wonders in the Apostolic age. But he could not believe that the Spirit's action was shut up to any one form of manifestation or that it had ever been withdrawn from the Church. The Holy Spirit appeared to him as the actually existing bond of every unity, whether domestic or social or ecclesiastical, a spirit which united men by bringing them into the fellowship of the Father and the Son; which spake by the prophets, but also in the conscience and higher reason of every man; who inspired the writers of the sacred books, but a Spirit also without whose constant presence and inspiration no man could think or perform those things that are good. Through his connection with the evangelical churches Maurice learned to identify the gospel of Christ with the proclamation of a message of deliverance from sin and guilt. He remained at heart an Evangelical all his days, but he also widened the range of Christ's redemptive work, till it included all other deliverances, from every form of oppression and tyranny, whether ecclesiastical, political, or social. In all this Maurice may appear as the pioneer in some method unknown before. But one is also impressed with that unbroken chain of spiritual influence by which the generations are bound together, handing on to those who follow the truth which has been received, waiting only till God shall provide the medium, the fitting soil in which the living seed at last shall germinate, take root, and spring upward and bring forth fruit an hundred fold.

In his intellectual development Maurice had the unusual advantage of taking the full course of study at Oxford first, and then at Cambridge. He caught the spirit, the subtle quality of each of the great universities which have stood throughout their history for differing ideals and tendencies in English thought. Cambridge has been the congenial home of spiritual largeness and freedom. There Puritanism found its stronghold in the sixteenth century, to be followed by the liberal school in the English Church of Cudworth, More, and Whichcote. It was at Cambridge that the Evangelical School was nourished, and to Cambridge belongs the honour of ranking Coleridge among its pupils. Oxford, on the other hand, which in the Middle Ages was more closely identified with the scholastic philosophy, has given birth to two great conservative movements, the Anglican revival under Laud in the seventeenth century, and again under Newman and Pusey, of which the tendency in both cases was to idealize or deify the existing institution as against the disintegrating forces of change or revolution. Maurice felt the historical appeal, the sense of historical continuity which Oxford cherishes, but the influence of Cambridge was the stronger. He imbibed there what may be called the spirit of Platonic realism, according to which the eternal idea or pattern of human things is always larger than its embodiment in any human institution and forever calls men to rise to its fuller appreciation. However visionary or impracticable the idea may seem, its deepest ground is invoked in the eternal will. Thus Maurice was led to insist upon the ideal constitution of the Church in Christ its head, as the actual reality, and not a mere spiritual aspiration which could rest in the background of thought. His conception of the Church, which brought him into conflict with what may be called an Aristotelian realism, divinizing the existing order as if change or improvement were but sacrilege, was throughout his life one of the ruling ideas of Maurice's theology. He preached it to the workingmen, he traced its presence in history, he urged it as the basis of Christian unity, he would have it carried to the heathen world as the solvent of its dark confusion — the brotherhood of human souls, a divine-human fellowship of which Christ was the head and leader, the Holy Spirit the bond of inward unity, the fatherhood of God its eternal ground in the infinite and sovereign will.

The man who wrought most powerfully upon Maurice after leaving the university was Coleridge, "the Master," as he has been called, "of those who know." Maurice did not come into personal contact with him, but the study of his life and his writings reconciled him to the Church of England, of which he became a minister, and, above all, taught him the significance of the doctrine of the Trinity. It was no longer an arithmetical puzzle as it had seemed to the typical mind of the last century, but the comprehensive formula of the Christian faith, which contained the reconciliation of the contradictions of speculative thought about the divine existence as well as the satisfaction of the deeper needs of the spiritual life. In the light of God as one and yet triune, the fellowships and relationships of earth were disclosed as having their ground and justification in the eternal fellowship which existed in the bosom of God. In this conviction the Christian Church had resisted the pressure of the imperial will in the ancient days of its alliance with the Roman Empire — that the Son of God who had assumed humanity in the body of this flesh was one and co-equal with the Father. And again in the strength of this conviction, the barbarism which overcame the Empire had in turn been overcome. It had also been the watchword of Christianity in the struggle with Islam when the seemingly difficult and complex idea of God had triumphed over a seeming simplicity, which was, after all, but an empty abstraction. But its historical interest and significance paled before its spiritual and moral appeal to the individual soul, or to social reformers rejecting the Church and disowning God. For the deep-seated and widespread scepticism of the age was assuming that God existed apart from human life, indifferent to human suffering, enforcing obligations and calling for sacrifices with which in Deity there could be no sympathy, for they were alien to the divine nature. But, in the name of God as Father, Son, and Holy Ghost, human relationships and duties and obligations of self-sacrifice were taken up, as it were, into God, and glorified by his inmost essential life. The divine became the prototype of the human; eternal fatherhood and sonship were the pattern from which the human relationship was derived, and not an analogy inferred from the human family. Sacrifice and suffering entered as an integral factor into the divine life, before it proceeded forth from God as the moral law of the universe. In the incarnation of God in Christ and in the atoning sacrifice on the cross was illustrated the identification of divine with human interests.

So great was the importance which Maurice attached to the doctrine of the triune name that in his book on "The Religions of the World" he applied it as the test by which they were to be measured and judged. Confucianism and Mohammedanism could not rise to the truth of the fatherhood of God because they lacked the knowledge of the Son, through whom alone fatherhood could be fully revealed. Brahminism abounded in incarnations of the divine, but they ended in themselves because the knowledge was wanting of the Eternal Father. Buddhism dreamed of an infinite Spirit in which all men shared, but because it did not know the Father and the Son its doctrine of the Spirit was void, as its highest goal was also reduced to Nirvana.

The ample learning which Maurice needed in order to illustrate and enforce the truth which he discerned, he had the opportunity to gain during the years from 1840 to 1853, when he held the professorship of history and literature in King's College in London. His books bear witness, and more particularly his "History of Philosophy" and his "Social Morality," to the thoroughness and depth of his acquaintance with systems of thought, or his insight into men and motives, or his power of interpreting literature and life. In these works we may read his appeal to the educated mind of his age. He does not offer new arguments for the divine existence, or endeavour to overcome scepticism by dialectics, but rather makes manifest how God is revealed in all the higher forms of human thought and expression. All history resolved itself before his eyes into a spiritual drama. The world everywhere appeared to him as bearing witness to God, as if it were fed with the life of God and shone with the light of God. But Maurice does not appear in his books or elsewhere in his work as if engaged or preoccupied with the anxious search for God. If he seems burdened, it is as if the weight of the divine revelation might overpower him. His attitude is that of receptivity for truth, or as if passivity were the condition for seeing and receiving. His experience confirms what Wordsworth had taught:

> Nor less I deem that there are powers
>   Which of themselves our minds impress;
> That we can feed this mind of ours
>   In a wise passiveness.
>
> Think you 'mid all this mighty sum
>   Of things forever speaking,
> That nothing of itself will come,
>   But we must still be seeking?

In addition to his other work, Maurice gave much of his time and thought to the improvement of the working classes. So identified was he with the cause of social reform that he became known as the father of Christian Socialism. He was the founder of a college for workingmen whose success was mainly owing to his disinterested labours. He had a lofty conception of the capacity of men engaged in physical toil and without education to receive the higher forms of truth and the results of learning. He aimed to overcome their peculiar scepticism as to whether God were doing anything for the emancipation of society from its oppression. It was the spirit of his teaching that it was God who was raising up the very reformers who disowned Him, that it was a divine spirit which stirred up social discontent as the condition of social progress.

While the thought of Maurice does not lend itself easily to brief summaries, yet it is not difficult to trace in all his writings one common element which binds them together in a consistent whole. That "religious realism" which enabled him to grasp the fatherhood of God as an actual relationship which could not be broken may be discerned in every attitude of his mind. He looked upon religious institutions, not as identical with their divine idea, but as witnesses to a higher reality. Because the reality existed independently of its acknowledgment, he could be charitable while holding the strongest convictions, dogmatic while rejoicing in the largest freedom of thought. What to the popular mind seemed like divine indifference to human affairs was to his mind the visible token of His presence. The religious doubt from which others fled in alarm, he welcomed as an aid to the deeper knowledge of God. Where others spoke of a lost and ruined world, he spoke of a world which had been redeemed by Christ. Some said that only those who had been baptized were the children of God; others, that to become a child of God one must have been converted and have the witness of an inward experience; he said that all men were children of God in virtue of their creation by the Eternal Father. Against those who maintained that religion was repugnant to the natural man, he affirmed religion to be that which the heart needed and for which it craved. In contrast with the method of those who laboured to overcome the natural depravity of the heart as the first step in religious experience, he preached the " God within," even to reprobates, as a divine appeal in order that they might claim the heritage of sonship. In the common thought the Church of God was identified with some existing institution; he regarded the institution as witnessing to the existence of the Church. The true Church did not require to be founded or carried, but to be proclaimed as having already an actual existence, the brotherhood of men in Christ. It was customary in speaking of the forms of human government to classify theocracy by itself, as if it had once existed among the Jewish people or been attempted as an experiment at various moments in history; but he maintained that theocracy, God's government, underlay all forms of human government as their pattern, the test by which they would be vindicated or condemned.

This reversal of ordinary judgments, to which men have become accustomed by long habit of training, constitutes a difficulty in reading Maurice which is not easily overcome — a difficulty akin to that which followed the Copernican discovery, when reality was placed in such strange contradiction to the testimony of the senses that it still requires an effort of the mind to adjust the seeming appearance with the actual fact. There was one inference which Maurice urged with great strenuousness — that in the spiritual world relationships were timeless, or could not be expressed in terms of quantity; that eternal life and eternal death were phrases charged with spiritual potency without reference to their duration. This contention regarding the use of the word "eternal" goes to the heart of the Maurician theology, affording a glimpse into a higher order, where things are not what they seem; where, instead of the divine revolving around the human, God becomes the central sun of an infinite spiritual universe in whom men live and move and have their being. The relationship of fatherhood and sonship constitutes the law of spiritual gravitation from which there is no escape, in whose glad recognition and obedience consists eternal salvation.

But, apart from his theological teaching, it is the supreme tribute to be paid to Maurice that he stood throughout his life as a confessor to his age, listening to the story of human doubt in deep sympathy, and never turning his ear away from any man who found difficulty in believing. Tennyson, who was his friend, has described him in what he did for himself and for others :

The faith, the vigour, bold to dwell
   On doubts that drive the coward back,
   And keen through wordy snares to track
Suggestion to her inmost cell.

He fought his doubts and gathered strength,
   He would not make his judgments blind,
   He faced the spectres of his mind
And laid them; thus he came at length

To find a stronger faith his own;
   And power was with him in the night,
   Which makes the darkness and the light,
And dwells not in the light alone.

It was the testimony of Archdeacon Hare, while Maurice was still alive, that no one had done so much in reconciling the reason and the conscience of the thoughtful men of the age to the faith of the Church: "It is in great measure owing to him that the intellect of the rising generation is with us rather than against us." In the words of another eminent contemporary, Dr. Montagu Butler: "Wherever rich and poor are brought closer together, wherever men learn to think more worthily of God in Christ, the great work that he has laboured at for nearly fifty years shall be spoken of as a memorial of him." He held no high preferment in the Church of England, but the world recognized him for what he was and for what he had done. At his death in 1872 there was a demonstration of public feeling which for spontaneity and universality had not been witnessed since the funeral of the Duke of Wellington. Beneath his bust in Westminster Abbey is recorded the only estimate we need: "He was not that light; but was sent to bear witness of that light."

XII

CAN WE BE PROPHETS?

XII

CAN WE BE PROPHETS?

BY THE VERY REV. F. W. FARRAR, D.D.

1. Can we be prophets? Most assuredly, yes. It is not the possibility which is wanting, but the will. We are called to be, every one of us in our degree and measure, prophets of the Lord; interpreters, that is, of his will to men, both on our lips and in our lives. It is, then, most important to us to meditate and understand what a prophet is, what he has to do, what he has to expect, what he may hope to achieve. What the prophet has to do is to sweeten the moral air which the world breathes; to raise the tone of society; to expose the hollowness of the compromises which the heart is constantly making with the powers of evil; to set forth an example of something higher and more heroical in religion than his age affects; to turn men's eyes from the dancing bubbles of avarice and ambition to the dis-

tant, the future, and the unseen ; to live as one to whom it has been granted to see the things that are invisible. This inscription was found carved over a temple door in a southern island : " The world was given us for our own upbuilding, not for the purpose of raising sumptuous houses; life, for the discharge of moral and religious duties, not for pleasurable indulgence; wealth, to be liberally bestowed, not avariciously hoarded ; learning, to produce good actions, not empty disputes." In other words, life is a serious and noble thing, and we are in daily danger — a danger to which most of us succumb — of making it a paltry, a petty, a frivolous, a dishonest, and a corrupted thing. And if God sends us prophets, it is that they may raise us up, that their words and deeds may breathe like a fresh wind through the perfumed and polluted atmosphere of society ; that they may become electric to flash through all the world the wholesome lightnings of truth and faith, startling the strongholds of immoral selfishness and shattering the refuges of accepted lies. And yet all this the prophet has to do, often alone ; often in deep obscurity and isolation ; often in the midst of poverty and persecution ; and he must do it with a deep

and crushing sense of his own feebleness and
imperfections, but making a loyal sacrifice of
his earthly life and his earthly hopes. How,
then, can we be prophets — we, the worldly;
we, the sensual; we, the idle and sluggish; we,
the vulgar and conventional; we, who worship
Mammon, and love pleasure, and delight so
much in scandal and hatred and lies? As
we are, we cannot be prophets; but are the
wings of six-winged seraphim — the twain with
which they did fly — folded forever? Is there
no temple more? Is heaven closed forever?
Burns there no fire on the altar? Has the
chariot of heaven ceased to descend to earth?
Are there no hot coals of fire to touch and
purify the unclean lips? Does the Lord say
no longer from his throne above the cherubim,
"Whom shall I send, and who will go for us?"
He who made the stammerer Moses his lawgiver, when he was in the wilderness but a
shepherd of alien sheep; He who made the
peasant Amos a prophet, as he earned his few
daily pence by gathering the coarse fruit of the
sycamore; He who made a prophet of Jeremiah when he was yet but a timid child; He
who slung a sword round the neck of the least
of the children of Manasseh, and sent him forth

to smite the innumerable foe — cannot He make sons of God and heroes of us, even of us? If the world summoned us to her splendours and her feasts, if some one offered us a life of ease and wealthy self-indulgence, what a rush there would be to claim it!

> Hark! rising to the ignoble call,
> How answers each bold Bacchanal!

But when God calls us and offers Heaven as the issue, will we all slink back in silence? Shall He alone find none to brave sorrow and loss for Him, among the many whom He has made? Well, He calls us now!

2. But God never deceives us. His prophets must be made of stern stuff, men of nerve and insight. He does not promise us any primrose path of dalliance. He says, "If ye would be my soldiers, ye must endure hardness. If ye would run in my race, ye must train. If ye would be my athletes, ye must deny yourselves. If ye are to be my prophets, then, like all my best and greatest prophets, in the world ye shall have tribulation." Why must this be so? It is, in one word, because the prophet must escape the average. The mass of mankind live the average life. They are easy-going, con-

ventional, traditional, commonplace. They do what others do; say what others say; they do not either think or act for themselves; any shibboleth does for them, so that it is current; any sophism suffices them, so it be accepted; they are but echoes; they pair off, as one has said, in insane parties, and because they ignore the deep realities of morals and religion, they detest to have their sand-built houses shaken, or their sluggish ease disturbed. It is almost incredible how hostile mankind has been to its greatest men. Scarcely ever has there been a great soul uttering truth but there has been the shadow of Calvary. It is because the majority do not like trouble, and to face new truth is a trouble. However much they may be told that there is no such word as *mumpimus*, still, like the old Catholic priest, they will refuse to change it for the right but unfamiliar *sumpsimus*. And that is why the world poisons Socrates, who bids it think out its own philosophy, and burns those who bid it amend its false religion. Majorities are constantly in the wrong. When Phocion heard the multitude applaud his speech, he turned round in surprise and asked, " Have I said anything wrong, then ? " " Always," as Goethe said, " it is the individual who works for progress, not the age. The ages have always been the same." It is this fact which robs of any cynical bitterness the saying of a great writer, that the world is composed of some thousand million human beings — mostly fools. Well, but the prophet must escape the average; he must not be a fool. Least of all must he be so in spiritual intuition and moral views.

3. Now, we cannot get to practical applications till we have grasped fundamental facts; we cannot do even small duties without the strength inspired by great principles. It requires a converted character to make even a thoroughly honest and satisfactory housemaid. It is not so easy as men seem to assume to be a Christian. To be a party religionist — to be an Evangelical, or a Broad Churchman, or a High Churchman — is very easy. But it is not easy to be a brave, true, honest man. Let me, then, try to illustrate what I have been saying. Let me try to show that no man can be truly good unless he escapes the average; to show that to escape the average costs something; and so, gradually, from great examples, to learn what to us is so inestimably precious and indispensable to learn; namely, how, with some courage

and some insight, to do our duty. Would God all the Lord's people were prophets; but we cannot be so by echoing common falsehoods and by running in conventional grooves. Let me show, by an instance, what the prophet must do and bear.

4. In the third century after Christ a boy was born at Alexandria, of Christian parents, in days of persecution. His parents trained him carefully, and he showed, even as a child, so bright a wisdom that, as he slept, the father would sometimes kiss reverently the breast of his sleeping son, whom he regarded as a temple of the Holy Ghost. Fierce persecution arose, and the father was seized and imprisoned. The boy, then but sixteen years old, showed such ardent longing for the crown of martyrdom that his mother had to conceal his clothes, and so prevent him from going forth into peril; yet, even then, he wrote to his father to be brave and not to shrink. The father was martyred. The boy, left with a mother and five brothers and sisters entirely destitute, toiled for their support. Being a prodigy of learning, he supported himself by teaching pupils, and then sold all his books of classic literature for an annuity of a few pence a day, on which,

throughout life, he lived. Taking the Gospel literally, he would have no shoes, and but one coat, and would touch no strong drink, and lived from boyhood in severe and noble simplicity. Almost before he was a man he became the head of the great catechetical school of Alexandria. Amid constant perils he lived a life which was, from first to last, one long prayer, one long struggle for closer union with the Eternal and the Unseen. He exercised on the Church of his own day, and of all succeeding ages, an almost incredible influence. He had saints and martyrs and holy hermits and wise bishops among his converts and pupils. He won over to the faith alike Christian heretics and heathen philosophers. He wrote hundreds of books and pamphlets which others, without acknowledgment, appropriated. He was, even by the confession of his enemies, the greatest man who had risen in the Church since the days of the Apostles, and perhaps also the holiest. His homilies have been the type of all homilies since. He laid the very foundation of the science of textual criticism. He was the first who attempted a philosophy of Christianity. After years of incredible labour and self-denial, in which he rendered to the Church such services as no man has ever rendered since, he died a martyr's death in the Deciæ persecution. That man was the great Christian Father, Origen the Adamantine. And what was his reward? In his lifetime, bitter envy, malignant persecution; after his death, the *damnamus* of Augsburg and the *anathema* of Rome. The splendour of his attainments raised him a host of enemies; the depth of his thoughts frightened the conventional ignorance which took itself for orthodox belief. This greatest and holiest of men was branded as a heretic nearly three centuries after his death by the combined intrigues of a cunning and worthless bishop and a cruel emperor. For centuries it continued to be debated whether he was not suffering infernal torments; and though, in the fifteenth century, when learning revived once more, and a ray of light out of God's eternity woke the Middle Ages from their dark and ghastly dream, when ancient Greece once more "started into life, but with the New Testament in her hand"—though, I say, since then the best and greatest have ever honoured the name of Origen, yet this is the man at whom, to this day, every raw sciolist and every full-fed Pharisee still thinks that he may cast a stone. Why? Because Origen was a prophet; he escaped the average; he is, even still, too great for their comprehension, too wide and deep and brave a thinker for the average mediocrity of common and cringing thought.

5. So fares the prophet on earth in matters of religion. It is the same in matters of science. At the beginning of the twelfth century after Christ a boy was born of a good family in Somersetshire, who grew up to be one of the greatest men whom the world has ever seen. Only about once in a century does God kindle the glory of an exceptional intellect; and, alas! whenever such a light is kindled, the world, which loves darkness, generally does its best to quench it; even as, in some dim cave, the birds which love the twilight will flap out an uplifted torch with their obscure wings; or as by night, in African wilds, the moths and beetles will quench with their dark carcasses the traveller's lamp. This boy, born in 1214, was the founder of experimental philosophy. To him is due the very dawn of that science which is now the glory and blessing of the world. Even in that age, besides science, he mastered Greek, Latin, Hebrew, and Arabic.

He was the earliest writer on chemistry in Europe. In his works he anticipated by three centuries the invention of the telescope, by four centuries the discovery of the laws of optics, by more than five centuries the invention of steam, suspension bridges, the diving-bell, and the balloon. At that time what is called the scholastic system was triumphant. It was thought that there was no knowledge to be had outside the pages of Aristotle. For a Christian teacher to run counter to this heathen philosopher was to be a heretic. The student I speak of went to Oxford, and in order to devote his life to knowledge he became a Franciscan monk. He soon discovered that the Oxford of his day was languidly feeding on the thistles of a mere verbal knowledge; and that there was less to learn from all Aristotle, and all his commentators, than was to be learned from one line on the broad page of the works of God. He wrote a book which he called his "greater work" to show what were the chief causes of human ignorance. They were, he said, these four: (1) Servile deference to authority; (2) traditionary habit; (3) the neglect to train the senses to observe; and (4) the disposition to conceal our ignorance, and make a show of our supposed knowledge. Truer words were never uttered, and they are as applicable to religion as to science, and now as they were then. Now, what happened to this splendid benefactor of humanity among the hidebound slaves of pseudo-orthodox tradition? Ignorance, malignity, folly, and that sort of animal stupidity shown by men of decided opinions which are based on nothing — against which even the gods fight in vain — led the dull monks and stupid religionists of his day to accuse him of magic and sorcery. He spent many years of his life in prison. He was insulted, scorned, and, it is believed, even tortured. That man was Roger Bacon, a far greater man than Francis Bacon, Earl of Verulam, by whom his fame has been eclipsed. It was not till the age of seventy that, broken in heart and broken by suffering, he was liberated from prison. In the last eight years of his life he was able to do nothing. He was driven to the bitter thought that men, as he knew them, were so base, so little, and so ignorant that they were not worth the pain and toil which he had endured on their behalf. God had inbreathed an intellect into one of his children which would have anticipated by three centuries the richest blessings which science has bestowed upon mankind. God kindled it; man quenched it. Truly, "however we brazen it out, we men are a little tried." Had there been no persecuted prophets to be loftier than the common run of us, we should have been low indeed.

6. I give these two instances to show that a man may be a prophet in many directions, but that if we hope, if we try, in any direction to escape the average, it will cost us something. It may cost us nothing less than the success and happiness of our lives. So that I hope that not one will say, "What is all this to me? I cannot be a great religious thinker like Origen, or a great scientific discoverer like Roger Bacon. I cannot lift mankind from the slough of intellectual sloth and moral compromise in which they love to lie." Pardon me; that is not quite true. We cannot be profound and learned like Origen, or men of superb genius like Roger Bacon, but every one of us can be humble like Origen, and brave like Origen, and unresentful like Origen; and candid, and thoughtful, and lovers of truth like Roger Bacon; and we, like them both — in great things or in little, as God shall grant to us — may help to improve the moral judg-

ments and to raise the moral standard of the world. To do this requires no mental greatness, no grand position. It has been done by youths and timid girls, by poor women and penniless, persecuted men. Many a poor woman or boy may think that what I have said was not for them, because they never heard so much as the names of these great men; well, but their names, and the age in which they lived, are of no consequence; what is of consequence is that they were just human beings, who breathed common air of life, who had once been little babes in the cradle as you and I were. In our own way, to our own degree, we can walk in their steps, as they walked in the steps of their Saviour Christ.

7. For, mark, it does not want genius or power or learning to benefit men by braving their false judgments, by scorning their hypocritical alliances with sin, by opening their eyes to the infamy of accepted customs. It only wants — if I may use a vulgar word — it only wants pluck; fidelity; moral manliness. It wants no knowledge beyond that of the Lord's Prayer and the Ten Commandments in the vulgar tongue. It only wants the eyes open to see God's law. Yet how marvellously rare

is this moral courage! Brute courage; instinctive courage; the courage of the tiger "which bounds with bare breast and unarmed claws upon the hunter's spear"; the flashy courage of the bully in the ring, or of the felon who, in his own brutal language, "wants to 'die game' upon the scaffold" — that is common enough; but the courage which dares to confront an angry king, or, standing up before a raging mob, dares to say, "You are wrong"; the courage which says, "I will not follow the multitude to be lost"; the courage which sees nothing but feebleness in the plea, "every one else does it, so I must do it too"; the courage of the man who, when standing up against brute force for law and right, says, "No bullets and no threats shall cow me in the clear direction of my duty"; still more the courage which can face and shame down a wrong custom amid the execrations of its votaries — that courage requires no genius except a moral genius which the most ignorant man or woman alive can show; and that moral genius of fearless rectitude is most astonishingly rare. We all know one memorable instance, to which I shall therefore but passingly allude. We know how, in ancient days, existed the horrible cruelty of public games in which criminals and gladiators — often barbarians — fought each other and stabbed each other to death before the yelling and gaping multitude. Who would have thought that such a custom would have survived no less than four centuries of Christianity? Yet it did; and we need not be so much surprised when we remember that our fathers looked on unmoved at the English brutalities of bear-baiting and cock-fighting; that dog-fighting still secretly survives, that there may be men even among my readers who have looked on at the foul and filthy spectacle of a prize-fight. But who stopped gladiatorial shows? Who wiped that infamy from the manners and morals of a nominally Christian Empire? Not emperors, or consuls, or lawyers, or writers of genius, or eloquent preachers, or learned divines, but just a rude, illiterate, unknown Asiatic monk, who had the courage to say, "This is wrong," and the courage to say, "So far as I am concerned, it shall not be." The show was going on; the myriads were assembled in the Coliseum; the gladiators were matched; the Emperor was in the chair; there was a clash of swords and a stream of blood, and the horrible spectacle had fairly begun. Then, in his monk's rude dress, down into the arena leaped the intrepid man, and, unarmed as he was, thrust himself between the weapons of that murderous struggle. It was the poor blind monk Telemachus. "Who is he? What presumptuous insolence! Down with him!" The mob hooted, yelled, raged, leaped over the barriers, hurled stones at him, would have rent him limb from limb. The very gladiators, whom he would have saved, turned their swords against him. He fell a mangled mass, beaten to death by innumerable blows. It is the only day of all his life of which a single fact is known. But what a day! it was a day in which his plain sense of right and wrong, his plain courage in acting up to it, had done nothing less than liberate the world!

> Sound, sound the trumpet; shrill the fife!
>   To all the sensual world proclaim,
> One crowded hour of glorious life
>   Is worth a world without a name!

8. Let me give another instance. It requires no small courage to resist the power and decrees of kings. It is never right to do so except when righteousness and truth demand, and one is sorry to see those high dear issues confused for

the sake of mere fantastic puerilities. When they do, when there is a clear collision between conscience and the civil power, no good man, no true man, no brave man, ought to flinch. Isaiah, we saw, did not flinch before Ahaz and Manasseh; nor Elijah before Jezebel; nor St. Ambrose before Theodosius; nor St. Chrysostom before Eudosia. Yet even Luther and Melancthon did before Philip of Hesse. John had said to Herod, with noble and blunt forthrightness, "It is not lawful for thee to have her"; yet Luther and Melancthon — though the shame of it afterwards almost broke Melancthon's heart — practically allowed Philip of Hesse to contract a bigamous marriage. Now we, thank God, are never likely, in any worthy or sensible cause, to come into collision with the civil power; but there is not one of us who may not have to confront some superior — our employer in an office, our master in a shop, if they bid us do wrong. And this may cost us much; and there is a tremendous temptation not to do it. Yet how invaluable to others one brave word, one brave act, may be! In the reign of James II., in 1683, the clergy were ordered to read a declaration which they held to be illegal. Even eminent laymen advised submission; and to refuse it was to brave a tyrant as unscrupulous and as cruel as he was narrow and bigoted. Bishop Sprat had the baseness to comply, and with pale face and shaking hands he read it in the Abbey amid the noise of the congregation as they indignantly crowded out. But fifteen London clergymen met to consider whether they should do it. They were inclined to yield, when Dr. Edward Fowler got up and said, "I must be plain. The question is quite simple. Let each man say yes or no. But I cannot be bound by the vote even of the majority. This declaration I cannot in conscience read." His courage fired the rest, carried the day, and saved England from a Popish tyranny. In four churches, only, of London was the order read. The father of John Wesley, then a curate in London, chose for his text that day the words, "Be it known unto thee, O King, that we will not serve thy gods, nor worship the golden image which thou hast set up."

9. This is to act in the spirit of a prophet. It is to see the truth plainly, and to act up to it boldly; to see the truth unblinded by the mists of self-interest or the cobwebs of casuistry; to act up to it though rulers may threaten and mobs may yell.

I will give another illustration in our own day. In the youth of many of us duels were still common. The statesmen of that time, the literary men of that time, had — many of them — been engaged in duels, as some living men of eminence have been. The custom was bad, as un-Christian, as anti-Christian as anything could be; it was "a mixture of fashion and revengefulness, of murder and suicide." And yet society, so far from condemning it, considered it a necessary institution; and every hot-blooded young fool who misunderstood a neighbour's remark thought himself entitled to demand what he called "satisfaction." Now, though this spirit of murderous resentment and this reckless disregard of human life stood utterly condemned before the bar of every moral law, it required a very brave man indeed to resist it. A story is told of one such brave man. An insulting adversary spat in his face. "Young man," he said, "if I could wipe your blood off my conscience as easily as I can wipe your insult off my face, I would strike you dead this moment." But the person who did more than any one to give the death-blow to this wicked and senseless custom in our day was a peer — the Earl of Shaftesbury — who stands foremost for his services to mankind. Years ago he received a challenge from some blustering opponent. Instead of accepting it, he wrote back a quietly contemptuous refusal, and sent the letters to the police court and the newspapers. After that the proposal to settle a quarrel by being shot at and shooting at some else — a mode of settlement which, though it did not stand above the level of the morality of the Ojibways, yet, simply because it was the custom of society, did not strike our grandfathers as grotesque or wrong — fell before the force of courage and insight into moral contempt and merited disgrace.

I have dwelt on these instances solely because the concrete is more likely to explain itself, more likely to act as a motive, than the abstract. And, not to talk only of distant and heroic things and persons of which history tells, I will give a very modern and every-day instance. The story has got into books; it has been told of various schools and other communities, but, as I tell it you, it was told me by one who knew, and was himself an actor in the scene. More than forty years ago, at a great English school (and in those days that state of things was common), no boy in the large dormitories ever dared to say his prayers. A young new boy — neither strong, nor distinguished, nor brilliant, nor influential, nor of high rank — came to the school. The first night that he slept in his dormitory not one boy knelt to say his prayers. But the new boy knelt down, as he had always done. He was jeered at, insulted, pelted, kicked for it; and so he was the next night, and the next. But, after a night or two, not only did the persecution cease, but another boy knelt down as well as himself, and then another, until it became the custom for every boy to kneel nightly at the altar of his own bedside. From that dormitory, in which my informant was, the custom spread to other dormitories, one by one. When that young new boy came to the school, no boy said his prayers; when he left it, without one act or word on his part beyond the silent influence of a quiet and brave example, all the boys said their prayers. The right act had prevailed against the bad custom and the blinded cowardice of that little world. That boy still lives; and if he had never done one good deed besides that deed, be sure it stands written for him in golden letters on the Recording Angel's book. Now, is not that kind of act an act which any one of us, from the richest statesman down to the youngest boy, might imitate? Are there no bad customs, no immoral conventions, no base acquiescences, no tolerated evils, in society? And if so, have you no share in them? Have you made no attempt to make a compromise between Christ and Belial? Are there no Temples of Rimmon in England? And, if so, have we never bowed in them? Well, whenever we see a wrong deed and have the courage to say, "It is wrong, and I, for one, will have nothing to do with it"; whenever we come in contact with a low and un-Christian standard, or a bad, unworthy habit, and are man enough first to refuse for our own part to succumb to it, and then to do our best to overthrow it — we are prophets. Indeed, those who live in poor streets have even more opportunities of taking this line and of making this stand than others have. If the Gospel means the example of our Lord Jesus Christ, remember that this is the Gospel and nothing but the Gospel, though it be not expressed in the shibboleths which Pharisees are most fond of writing on their broad phylacteries. For this — to see sin, which tried to pass itself off for virtue;

to expose hypocrisy, which wore the garb of religion; to save society, which was perishing of its own hidden corruption; to teach truth, though men hated it; to scatter darkness, though men loved it; to reveal the God of Love, though men had represented him as a Moloch of hatred; to teach men that their work in life was to love and to help their fellow-men, and so (and not by mere exclusive formulæ and malignant orthodoxies) to save their own souls — this, this emphatically, was the work of Christ. His work and therefore our work, for which he will inspire the courage. Be brave, be just, be truthful and honest to the heart's core, and so serve your brother man, and so serve best your Father God, and your Saviour the Lord Christ. If those be not lessons of the Gospel of the Pharisees, they are, ten thousand fold more than a gloomy Calvinism or a sectarian shibboleth, the lessons of the Gospel of Christ. "There are," a great statesman said, "there are steeps of Alma on the field of duty no less than on the field of blood." The question is, will we be one of the vulgar throng that will not face them, or will we be individual soldiers, however humble, in the "thin red line" that carries them against the foe ? If of the latter, then God will make us, too, his prophets, and will say to us, as to Ezekiel :

"And thou, son of man, be not afraid of them. Be not afraid of their faces ; be not afraid of their words, though briers and thorns be with thee, and thou dost dwell among scorpions."

THE END

www.ingramcontent.com/pod-product-compliance
Lightning Source LLC
Chambersburg PA
CBHW020807230426
43666CB00007B/901